Robert S. Hawker, Alfred Wallis

The poetical works of Robert Stephen Hawker, M.A.,

Sometime Vicar of Morwenstow, Cornwall: edited from the original manuscripts and annotated copies - together with a prefatory notice and bibliography

Robert S. Hawker, Alfred Wallis

The poetical works of Robert Stephen Hawker, M.A.,
Sometime Vicar of Morwenstow, Cornwall: edited from the original manuscripts and annotated copies - together with a prefatory notice and bibliography

ISBN/EAN: 9783337731533

Printed in Europe, USA, Canada, Australia, Japan

Cover: Foto ©ninafisch / pixelio.de

More available books at **www.hansebooks.com**

THE POETICAL WORKS OF
ROBERT STEPHEN HAWKER, M.A.

AT MORWENSTOW, 1896.

Rich-hearted minstrel of a wilder day!
   On these bleak hills thy harp is heard no more:
   The voice is hush'd that rang thro' ocean's roar
To foil the baffled billows of their prey.
Poet and priest!   To cheer the stranger's way;
   Or grant him, lonely boon, an alien grave,
   And bless with burial whom thou could'st not save;
To be the poor man's friend; to set thy lay
   To music of the solitary sea—
This was thy dear ambition and thy fame:
   These craggy combes are consecrate to thee,
And ocean rolls an echo of thy name.
Thy memory needeth no recording hand:
Thou shalt "not be forgotten in this land."

C. E. B.

THE POETICAL WORKS

OF

ROBERT STEPHEN HAWKER, M.A.

SOMETIME VICAR OF MORWENSTOW, CORNWALL

EDITED FROM THE ORIGINAL MANUSCRIPTS
AND ANNOTATED COPIES

TOGETHER WITH A

PREFATORY NOTICE AND BIBLIOGRAPHY

BY

ALFRED WALLIS

JOHN LANE, THE BODLEY HEAD
LONDON AND NEW YORK
1899

"I would not be forgotten in this land."

Quest of the Sangraal, p. 171.

MORWENSTOW CHURCH.

FOREWORDS.

THE works of the Reverend Robert Stephen Hawker, of Morwenstow, first saw the light many years ago in the pages of publications of a more or less ephemeral character; and, although collections, both of his verse and prose, have been made from time to time by himself, and, since his death, by others, those volumes, like the originals, have become exceedingly scarce, whilst the interest attaching to them in the public mind has been strengthened, rather than weakened, through the lapse of time. Of the poems, "The Trelawny Ballad," or "Song of the Western Men," is perhaps the best known, owing to the controversy respecting its authorship, which has lasted down to the present day, and in which such literary giants as Sir Walter Scott and Lord Macaulay once took part. As will be shown, however, there can be no doubt whatever that the song as it is now known was evolved by Mr. Hawker out of the burden, or refrain, of some lost ditty (one that, for anything we know, may have been chaunted by the Cornish miners two centuries ago), much as Professor Owen performed his feats of organic restoration by the aid of a fragment of bone. Many of his other poems have also proved themselves thoroughly "popular"—having been read again and again, in public, and included in many books of poetical "Selections" and "Treasuries"—and it is therefore believed that a new and comprehensive edition will be welcomed not only in the West of England, where his name has long been a household word, but throughout the world of literature, in which his voice was once recognised as one that brought with it the echo of the singer's own strong feelings of love for God and man, conveyed in tones at once strong and piercing, yet most melodious to the ear. I have endeavoured to arrange the scattered songs so as to indicate the period, and, to some extent, the circumstances in which they were composed; and the *Bibliography* will, I hope and believe, prove serviceable to collectors of first editions.

A. W.

Exeter, November, 1898.

MEMOIR.

A BRIEF record of the life of a clergyman whose personality is, in the memory of all who knew him, of so marked and individual a character, may fitly serve as usher to the literary exercises which were the outcome of his thoughts and feelings, sometimes tender and solemn in their tone and often sparkling with genuine wit and humour. No pretention to a formal biography, however, can be made here; nor is it necessary to deal otherwise than superficially with the opening and closing stages of the Vicar of Morwenstow's life-history. To the world at large, his writings speak for him—in that lesser sphere where amongst his humble folk he lived and moved and had his being, no mere words are needed to keep his memory green—his good deeds, and unselfish life of duty to God and man will not soon be forgotten on that rocky shore of St. Morwenna, which was the chief scene of his ministrations for upwards of forty years!

Robert Stephen Hawker was born at Plymouth on the 3rd of December, 1803; his father, Jacob Stephen

Hawker, was a medical practitioner who subsequently took Holy Orders, and was for many years Vicar of Stratton, North Cornwall. To Dr. Robert Hawker, his grandfather, the well-known Calvinistic minister (for half-a century Vicar of Charles Church, Plymouth), young Hawker was sent for education, but after some experience of private schools (where he was placed at the expence of his aunt, Mrs. Hodgson) he, being about 16 years of age, was sent to the Grammar School, Cheltenham, and here the bent of his poetic genius asserted itself in a volume of poems entitled " Tendrils, by Reuben," printed in an octavo volume dated 1821,* and reprinted at the end of the present collection.

From Cheltenham, he passed to Oxford, and entered at Pembroke in 1822; but, the death of his aunt occurring shortly afterwards, it became necessary for him to consider his position in the world, as his father was unable to bear, unassisted, the expenses of his University career. The result was that he proposed to, and was accepted by, Miss Charlotte Eliza I'Ans, one of the four daughters of Colonel Wrey I'Ans, of Whitstone House, Bude-Haven, a lady who, although many years his senior, was highly educated and accomplished, and who, besides being in sympathetic accord

---

* Dr. Lee says (*Memorials*, p. 64): "His earliest volume, published at Plymouth in 1825, was entitled ' Poetical First Buds. By Reuben.'" This is a fair sample of the "facts" upon which Dr. Lee's biography is constructed.— ED.

with his hopes and ambitions, was possessed of the means which would enable him to continue his studies at the University. It may, therefore, be said that, putting disparity of years out of the question, this lady was in every way a fitting helpmeet for an enthusiastic scholar. In consequence of his marriage, which took place on November 6, 1824, his name was removed from Pembroke to Magdalen Hall, whither his wife accompanied him.

In the year 1825, during the Long Vacation spent near Bude, Mr. Hawker wrote the famous "Song of the Western Men" (known also as "The Trelawney Ballad"), whilst sitting, as he himself has written, "under a stag-horned oak in Sir Beville Granville's Walk in Stowe Wood." The ballad was sent anonymously to *The Royal Devonport Telegraph and Plymouth Chronicle*, and printed in the issue of September 2, 1826. The following year, 1827, he gained the Newdigate Prize with his poem entitled "Pompeii," and this circumstance led indirectly to his subsequent preferment to the living of Morwenstow, by bringing him under the notice of Dr. Philpotts, afterwards Bishop of Exeter. In a letter to his friend Mr. J. G. Godwin, written in 1862, he gives the following interesting narrative :—

"When I won 'Pompeii' it was the first year after the limit of fifty lines was taken off. H. Exon (then Rector of Stanhope) had told William [his son] to be sure and bring home with him the Prize 'Newdigate.'

He carried mine with him, and his father read it aloud to the family that evening. When he came to Exon (Bishop) he said to me, 'It gives me real delight to find your name entered in the diocese-book by Bishop Carey for early preferment.' Now, I should tell you that I was ordained Deacon by Bishop Carey, and that the examining chaplain, Bartholomew, so reported of me that I had to read the Gospel in the Ordination Service, and in my interview with the Bishop, he said 'We don't give livings to men who write prize poems, Mr. Hawker, unless they pass examinations such as you have passed also.' I, in my vain-glory, thought this a very emphatic kind of praise, and I commit it to you for converse in the growing generation when I am not."

Mr. Hawker took his B.A. degree in 1828, and, being ordained Deacon in 1829, when 25 years of age, was appointed to the Curacy of North Tamerton in Devonshire. His life here was uneventful, but marked, no doubt, with hard work. He received Priest's Orders in 1831, at the hand of the Bishop of Bath and Wells, and proceeded to his M.A. degree in 1836. Whilst dwelling at North Tamerton, in 1832, he published at Oxford the first series of his *Records of the Western Shore*, poems, chiefly legendary, connected with Devon and Cornwall, the second series of which appeared in a volume of " Poems " printed at Stratton in 1836. Most of these ballads were republished in *Ecclesia : a Volume of Poems*, Oxford, 1840, and in *Cornish Ballads*, 1869, reprinted in 1884.

In 1834 the living of Morwenstow was offered to Mr. Hawker in the following letter.

"Exeter, 15th December, 1834.

"My dear Sir,
 "The Vicarage of Moorwinstow,* in your own neighbourhood, being vacant, I would offer to present you to it, did I not think that it is not a parish suited to you. I would rather see you placed in some district where access to congenial society would be easy to you, and where you would be fully appreciated, and by being more in tune with things around you, would also be more useful, with God's blessing, to others. I have not however bestowed the living elsewhere, so that if I am mistaken about you (which after our last conversation is not likely), inform me by an early post.
 "I am, my dear Sir,
   "Your faithful Friend and Bishop,
       "H. Exeter.
"Rev. R. S. Hawker."

Notwithstanding the Bishop's doubts whether so remote and solitary a parish as Morwenstow would be suitable to him, Mr. Hawker accepted the living, and went to reside there in January, 1835. He found a wilderness; for nearly a century there had been no resident parson. Mr. Young, the previous Vicar, who died in 1834, was non-resident, the parish having been served by a succession of curates, most of them also non-resident, and the vicarage was occupied by the parish clerk; it could scarcely be called a residence, for the roof leaked, which made it almost uninhabitable. Mr. Hawker rebuilt the house at his own cost, as

---

* The name of the village is thus spelt upon an old map of Devon and Cornwall in the possession of the Editor.

the Ecclesiastical Commissioners, upon some very shallow pretext, refused him any aid; he also built a school-house in the centre of the scattered parish, in order that it might be accessible to the children from all the surrounding hamlets. Besides these acts he caused the bridge in the valley of Combe (called "King William's Bridge," the King having contributed £20 to the undertaking) to be constructed over a dangerous ford; and, in 1843, he successfully contested the claim of the late Lord Churston (then Sir J. Buller) to a piece of church-glebe wherein springs the Well of Saint John—from which source, in his day, the water for the Sacrament of Baptism was always drawn. By his action in this matter, three-quarters of an acre of land was added to the glebe of 70 acres, which after his death was found to be a well-arranged farm, hedged and fenced, and supplied with good barns and out-buildings.

Upon his church of Saint Morwenna, the Vicar expended much of his income and all the energy of his loving care. Everywhere in his *Poems* will be found touching evidences of his delight in the ancient shrine of which he had been constituted the guardian, and of his veneration for the memory of the Saint herself.

In 1851 he became Curate of Welcombe, a Devonshire parish in the gift of Lord Clinton, neighbouring upon Morwenstow (which lies at the extreme north-eastern point of the county of Cornwall); and for the future he rode his pony (or, in later years, drove) to Welcombe and held a service at half past two, with very occasional exceptions, every Sunday afternoon, returning for evensong to Morwenstow. He seems to have acted as the postman for Welcombe, and was generally required to read his parishioners' letters and very frequently to answer them also.

And so his round of life went on in peaceful, but earnest, work; in assisting the poor under his charge; in reverent burial of the ship-wrecked dead whom the sea cast up upon the iron-bound coasts of his parish; in succouring survivors from the wrecks; and in striving manfully to do his duty under all sorts of adverse circumstances, whilst only allowing himself the recreation of poetry very occasionally.

On the 2nd of February, 1863, Mrs. Hawker died. She has been described as a woman of poetical, refined mind, with a strong sense of humour and possessed of sound judgment and discretion. She was a good German scholar, and I think it at least probable (in the absence of direct proof) that the translations from Schiller and Göthe given in the present volume may be accredited to her. She is known to have written the poem entitled "The Wreck," which is printed without comment in *Ecclesia*, but which is denoted in Mr. Hawker's copy of that work, in his own hand, as being "*by C. E. H.*" For some time before her death she became blind, and nothing, it is said, could be imagined more exquisitely touching than the constant attention and affectionate ministrations of her husband. After her death, Mr. Hawker fell into a condition of extreme depression which culminated in brain-fever, from which he recovered with difficulty.

Another important change in life, however, now awaited him. In 1863, his friend, the Rev. W. Valentine, came to reside at Chapel House in his parish, bringing with him, in the capacity of governess to his children, Miss Pauline A. Kuczynski, the daughter (by an English wife) of Count Kuczynski, a Polish noble, who having been obliged, for political reasons, to leave his native land, had taken refuge in this country under the protection of the British government. Mr. Hawker made the acquaintance of this lady of high birth and refinement, proposed to her and was accepted. They were married in December, 1864, and in the month of November in the following year a daughter was given to them, who was baptised by the glad father (his first marriage was childless) by the name of Morwenna Pauline. Two other daughters, born respectively in 1867 and 1869, were named Rosalind and Juliot, the latter in remembrance of a sister of St. Morwenna who had a cell and founded a church near Boscastle. His widow has recorded that "his children were a great joy to him, but at the same time a grave anxiety, for, with the exception of a life-policy for £1000, his resources did not admit of any provision being made for those who should survive him."

There can be no doubting the fact that this deep and grave anxiety did weigh, most heavily, upon Mr. Hawker's mind during the close of his useful life. His biographers (however widely they may differ concerning other circumstances relating to this period) concur in remarking upon the visible effect of that cloud which was incessantly hovering over him and his loved ones. In the year 1873, his health began seriously to fail, and a visit to London, undertaken in 1874, only temporarily benefited him.

"In the Spring of 1875," Mrs. Pauline Hawker writes, "rest and change were imperative, and we left Morwenstow on the 21st of June for the residence of his brother, Mr. Claude Hawker, at Boscastle, whence, after a visit of a week, we moved to Plymouth. The 9th of August was fixed for our return home; but on that day a clot of blood settled in the artery of the left arm* and he gradually sank, expiring on the morning of the 15th August. On the previous night, he was received into the Roman Catholic Church." Mr. Hawker was in fact buried at Plymouth with the ceremonials of the Roman Catholic Church, and his tombstone records the event.

Into the controversy to which this circumstance gave rise, it is not within the present writer's province to enter. Full biographies of the Vicar of

---

* This stoppage of the radial artery was an indication of organic affection of the valves on the left side of the heart, and of mechanical obstruction, leading to effusion on the brain, which was probably the cause of death.—ED.

Morwenstow have been published, for which the Rev. Sabine Baring-Gould and the Rev. Frederick George Lee are respectively responsible, and to them the attention of such of our readers as may be desirous of more information upon the subject than may be given here is directed. Concerning the man himself there can be only one opinion. His contemporaries agree unanimously in praising his strong human sympathies; his beautiful unselfishness, displayed unconsciously in all his actions; his never-failing charity towards all who, dead or living, needed his aid; his deep devotion to his Master, and his strict observance of the line of duty which, in all honour and honesty, he had marked-out early in life for his own guidance, and which he followed to the very end. These were his traits of personal character; they are visible in his poetry, they are recorded in the hearts of those who loved him, and through them his worth will be estimated by posterity.

Mr. Hawker's poetical career must have commenced very early in life. Mr. Baring-Gould has told us of an amusing instance of his having "altered and amended" his grandfather's well-known hymn, "Lord, dismiss us with thy blessing," and of his recommending the "improved version" to the favourable notice of the angry author, as being "much better" (which, indeed, may be said to be the case); an escapade which resulted in his being sent away to school. It was at Cheltenham School that his first volume of poems, entitled "Tendrils; by Reuben;" was committed to the press; but the present writer, whilst searching recently in the files of the *English Chronicle and Whitehall Evening Post*, has accidentally discovered in the issue for Sept. 8th, 1821, the following verses, which are given here in order that they may be compared with those which under the same heading were subsequently published in "*Tendrils*":—

THE FADED ROSE.

"One fatal Remembrance."

I do remember, in a lovely spot
  (Whose very beauty might well be forgot),
There was a Rose of Nature's choicest growth;
  Such as the night-bird seeks, and makes her bower;
The breeze would sigh around it, as 'twere loth
  To bear the perfume from so sweet a flower.
The dew of Heaven loved it—and the ray
  Of evening lingered for its latest smile;
Yet would have deem'd that it *could not* decay,
  So lov'd, so sweetly nurtur'd; but the guile
Of autumn night-winds stole its bloom away.
It died, and the morning found a dewy gem,
Hung as in mockery, on the wither'd stem!
  And there was *one*, a lonely, lovely one,
Who faded like that rose—the worm of grief,
  Of soul-hid sorrow, that was told to none,
Of every bitterness that mocked relief,
  Prey'd on that lovely flower, and leaf by leaf
It fell to nothingness.
          Some thought she strove
With that unslumbering serpent, blighted love!
                  REUBEN.

This discovery makes it certain that young Hawker made his first bow before a London audience, and it is also worthy of remark that the London evening paper in question was by no means addicted to the cultivation of minor poets, for, with the exception of some lines headed " Midnight," and signed " Albert," which appeared a few weeks later, " Poet's Corner " in that journal is conspicuous by its vacuity.

A bibliography of Mr. Hawker's printed poetry follows; but his habit of sending detached verses as contributions to various magazines, and of circulating "leaflets" amongst his parishioners and friends, has rendered the task of compilation not a little difficult. Some of them are registered in *Bibliotheca Cornubiensis*; and Dr. Brushfield, M.D., whose kindness in lending his " Hawker Collections " for the purposes of this edition we gratefully acknowledge, has noted others. We have, where practicable, indicated these sources within brackets at the end of the various poems. *Willis's Current Notes*, an extinct periodical of the *Notes and Queries* order, was greatly affected by Mr. Hawker, and he also sent contributions, both prose and verse, to *The Gentleman's Magazine, Household Words, All the Year Round, Notes and Queries, Belgravia, The Lamp*, and other periodicals.

It only remains to be added that a biography of this remarkable man, whose strong individuality and mental power are impressed indelibly upon his poetical works, is a *desideratum*. His *Poems*, it is true, speak for him in language that is entirely his own, scarcely needing any interpreter other than such notes as he himself deemed necessary for the elucidation of certain passages. But Mr. Hawker's life-history is one that is full of interest, and the somewhat ignoble war that breaks out occasionally over the incidents that unfortunately marked its termination, is too sad for the contemplation of those who revere his memory. As a Priest of the Church of England, he was honest, conscientious, and sincere; as a man, just and upright in all his dealings with mankind; and as a poet, few writers of our own day can equal him. None can claim a better title to the esteem, and even affection, of those who will only know him through the medium of his works.

MORWENSTOW VICARAGE.

BIBLIOGRAPHY OF THE POETICAL WORKS OF THE REV. R. S. HAWKER, M.A.

(Compiled by the Editor.)

TENDRILS. | BY REUBEN. | — | —"Poets are a sensitive race, whose sweetness is not to be | drawn forth, like that of the fragrant grass near the Ganges, by | crushing and trampling upon them." | LALLA ROOKH. | — | Cheltenham: | PRINTED BY S. Y. GRIFFITH, CHRONICLE OFFICE. | PUBLISHED BY HATCHARD AND SON, AND G. WHITAKER, LONDON ; | BULGIN, BRISTOL ; NETTLETON AND SON, PLYMOUTH ; | BETTISON, WILLIAMS, AND ROBERTS, CHELTENHAM. | 1821. 12mo. Blue paper-boards; printed label, "Tendrils." (*Collation copy*, Dr. Brushfield's.)

COLLATION :—Half-title, title, preface (dated "Charlton, 1821"). Dedication = 4 leaves, B to M, in fours (M 4 blank); or, pp. viii. (i. blank) + 86 + 1 blank. Colophon :—"S. Y. Griffith, Printer, Chronicle Office, Cheltenham."

*** This is Mr. Hawker's first published work, and is exceedingly scarce. The poem, "To a Faded Flower," first appeared in the *English Chronicle* for September 8th, 1821, a fact which is now made known for the first time.

POMPEII. | A PRIZE POEM ; | RECITED IN THE THEATRE, OXFORD, | JUNE THE TWENTY-SEVENTH, | M.DCCC.XXVII. | 12mo. Paper covers. (*Collation copy*, Dr. Brushfield's.)

COLLATION:—Twelve leaves, paged 1 to 22, the last leaf being an advertisement of "Oxford English Classics." On back of title: 𝔓rinted by D. A. Talboys, ®xford." Colophon:—"PRINTED BY D. A. TALBOYS, OXFORD." Again, in *Oxford English Prize Poems* (same printer), 1828.

Reprinted with *Records of the Western Shore*, Second Series, 1836; in *Ecclesia: a Volume of Poems*, 1840; *Echoes from Old Cornwall*, 1846; *Cornish Ballads*, 1869 and 1884; *Poetical Works* (Godwin), 1879; *South Devon Monthly Museum*, Sept., 1834.

*** There is a curious "advertisement" prefixed to the volume of *English Prize Poems*, noticed above:—

"This new edition of the OXFORD ENGLISH PRIZE POEMS owes its appearance to the following circumstances. The publisher, having bought the copyright of the last prize poem, POMPEII, expected, as a matter of course, to reap the full benefit of his purchase. Such, however, has not been the case, the proprietors of the last edition of this collection having pirated and annexed it to their volume. The publisher, without doubt, might, by legal proceedings, have procured redress for this attack upon his property; but he has chosen rather to repay them in kind by printing the whole collection. The public will benefit by the competition.
Oxford, Jan. 14, 1828."

RECORDS | OF | THE WESTERN SHORE. | BY | ROBERT STEPHEN HAWKER. | THE MEANING OF THE WORD CORNWALL IS, THE ROCKY | LAND OF STRANGERS. | NORDEN. | OXFORD, D. A. TALBOYS. | 1832. Fcap. 8vo. Wrapper, uncut.

COLLATION:—Title, Preface (dated "NORTH TAMERTON, June 1, 1832"). Dedication (Three stanzas "𝔗o 𝔒harlotte," the author's first wife). The Poems, pp. 7 to 56. Colophon: "OXFORD: PRINTED BY TALBOYS AND BROWNE." (*Collation copy*, Mr. A. Wallis's.)

*** "The Song of the Western Men" first appears, with the writer's acknowledgment, in this very rare little volume. It had been previously printed in *The Royal Devonport Telegraph and Plymouth Chronicle* for Sept. 2, 1826, and was reprinted at the private press of Davies Gilbert, Esq., at Eastbourne. [These copies have not been seen by the present writer.]

POEMS : | CONTAINING | *THE SECOND SERIES* | OF | RECORDS OF THE WESTERN SHORE. | 𝔉irst 𝔈dition. | *THE FIRST SERIES* | 𝔖econd 𝔈dition. | AND | POMPEII. | THE OXFORD PRIZE POEM FOR MDCCCXXVII. | BY | THE REVEREND R. S. HAWKER, M.A. | VICAR OF MORWENSTOW, CORNWALL. | FIT AUDIENCE FIND, THOUGH FEW. | MILTON. | PUBLISHED BY J ROBERTS, STRATTON. | 1836. | Post 8vo. Watered cloth. (*Collation copy*, Mr. J. G. Commin's.)

COLLATION :—The *Second Series of Records* contains pp. 1 to 52, including the general title and preface : The *First Series of Records*, Second Edition, contains pp. 1 to 56, including title and preface ; *Pompeii* contains pp. 22, including title, dedication (to Arthur Kelly, Esq.), and half-title ; lastly. a leaf advertising " By the same Author : Poems containing the First and Second Series of Records of the Western Shore." The cloth binding of the collation copy contains a printed leaf (p. 16) of the " Poems " in a smaller *format*, of which this seems to be a solitary specimen ; pages 15-16 have been reprinted owing to an error in the metre of one line— the present copy contains both the cancel and the reprint. Colophon : " Printed by J. Roberts, Stratton." The preface is dated " Morwenstow, July 1, MDCCCXXXVI.," and states that the book is published " for the benefit of my Parochial School."

Writing in 1853, Mr. Hawker laments that "he has not, and cannot obtain the volume published for him by Roberts, of Stratton, in 1836."

MINSTER CHURCH ; | AND | THE CONFIRMATION DAY. | AUG. XVII., M.DCCC.XXXVI. | 4to.

A *brochure* of six leaves, printed for private distribution. [We have not seen this.] It is reprinted in *Ecclesia*, 1840.

A WELCOME | TO | THE PRINCE ALBERT, | SUBMITTED TO THE QUEEN | ON THE APPROACH OF | HER MAJESTY'S MARRIAGE. | BY THE AUTHOR OF | POMPEII, | THE OXFORD ENGLISH PRIZE POEM FOR 1827. | — | OXFORD :—PRINTED BY T. COMBE, PRINTER TO THE UNIVERSITY. | SOLD BY TALBOYS, OXFORD ; RIVINGTONS, LONDON ; HANNAFORD, EXETER ; | NETTLETON, PLYMOUTH ; AND CATER, LAUNCESTON. | MDCCCXL. | Royal 8vo. Printed wrapper (as above). (*Collation copy*, Dr. Brushfield's.)

COLLATION :— Eight leaves; the poem ends on p. 7 with the signature, "*R. S. Hawker*," and date, "*The Vicarage, Morwenstow,* January 8th, 1840."

⁎ From a letter, in Dr. Brushfield's collection, addressed "To the Editor of the *Times*," by Mr. Hawker, dated June 19th, 1840, it appears that he sent two separate copies with a personal request that the poem might be noticed in *The Times*; Dr. Brushfield has endorsed the letter, "It was not published in *The Times*." However, in Mr. Hawker's own copy of *Ecclesia*, now before us, he has scored out this poem with vigorous cross strokes of his pencil, and appended his own idea of its value, thus:—"*Trash!!*"

ECCLESIA: | A VOLUME OF POEMS; | BY THE | REV. R. S. HAWKER, M.A. | VICAR OF MORWENSTOW, CORNWALL, AUTHOR OF "POMPEII," THE | OXFORD PRIZE POEM FOR M.DCCC.XXVII. | — | "If I forget thee, O Jerusalem, let my right hand forget her cunning. If I | do not remember thee, let my tongue cleave to the roof of my | mouth; yea if I prefer not Jerusalem in my mirth." | OXFORD: | Printed by T. Combe, Printer to the University; | SOLD ALSO BY J. G. AND J. RIVINGTON, ST. PAUL'S CHURCH- | YARD, AND WATERLOO PLACE; TALBOYS, OXFORD; | HANNAFORD, EXETER; LIDDELL, BODMIN; | AND NETTLETON, PLYMOUTH. | M.DCCC.XL. | 8vo. boards, or watered cloth, with paper label on back—"Poems. | by the | Rev. R. S. | Hawker. | — | Oxford, | M.DCCC.XLI." | (*Collation copy,* Mr. A. Wallis's.)

COLLATION :—(Title within "rules" is B1.) B to K in eights, or pp. 144, including title and final index-leaf. Four leaves of a list of "New Books in the course of publication by J. G. F. & J. Rivington," dated "January, 1841," precede the title-page.

⁎ In Mr. Hawker's own copy he has written on p. 95 (beneath the title to "The Wreck"), "*by C. E. H.*," the initials of his first wife. A second edition is said to have been published by Rivingtons in 1841; we do not believe this statement, and it will be observed that the above, first, edition bears the date 1840, upon the title, and 1841 upon the label at the back.

A. 𝕽𝖊𝖊𝖉𝖘 | SHAKEN WITH THE WIND. | BY THE | REV. R. S. HAWKER, M.A. | VICAR OF MORWENSTOW, CORNWALL; AUTHOR OF "ECCLESIA," ETC. | — | LONDON: | JAMES BURNS, 17, PORTMAN STREET, PORTMAN SQUARE. | — | 1843. | 12mo. green cloth, uncut edges, lettered on side "𝕽𝖊𝖊𝖉𝖘 | SHAKEN WITH THE WIND."

COLLATION :—Pp. 48 (all counted). The *collation copy* (Miss Hawker's) is imperfect. Mr. Hawker has struck his pen across the first stanza of *The Second Birth of the Princess Royal of England*, p. 5, and marked it " *Trash. R. S. H.*" The printers' names, Levey, Robson, and Franklyn, are on the reverse of the title, and as colophon after "The End."

B 𝕽𝖊𝖊𝖉𝖘 | SHAKEN WITH THE WIND. | THE SECOND CLUSTER ; | BY | THE VICAR OF MORWENSTOW, | CORNWALL. | Kowsa nebaz, ha kowsa da.] *Old Cornish Saying.* | — | DERBY, | HENRY MOZLEY AND SONS ; | AND JAMES BURNS, PORTMAN STREET, LONDON. | — | 1844. | 12mo. Green cloth, uncut. (*Collation copy*, Miss Hawker's.)

COLLATION :—Pp. 52 (all counted). Colophon :—" Henry Mozley and Sons, Printers, Derby." Lettered on side, as above, with addition, "THE SECOND CLUSTER."

⁎ These tiny volumes are of great interest and rarity.

THE POOR MAN | AND | HIS PARISH CHURCH | BY | 𝕿𝖍𝖊 𝖁𝖎𝖈𝖆𝖗 𝖔𝖋 𝕸𝖔𝖗𝖜𝖊𝖓𝖘𝖙𝖔𝖜, | CORNWALL. | — | 𝖘𝖊𝖈𝖔𝖓𝖉 𝕰𝖉𝖎𝖙𝖎𝖔𝖓. | PLYMOUTH : | EDWARD NETTLETON, WHIMPLE STREET, | PRINTER TO HER MAJESTY. | 1843. | 8vo. pamphlet, in paper covers. (*Collation copy*, Dr. Brushfield's.)

COLLATION :—Four leaves (all counted). The pages, numbered to vii., are within ruled borders. Colophon:—" 𝕿𝖍𝖊 𝕱𝖊𝖘𝖙𝖎𝖛𝖆𝖑 𝖔𝖋 𝕾𝖙. 𝕵𝖔𝖍𝖓 | 𝕿𝖍𝖊 𝕭𝖆𝖕𝖙𝖎𝖘𝖙, 1843." |

⁎ We have never seen a copy of this pamphlet (1843) without the words "second edition" on the title-page. It was printed, next, in the second cluster of "Reeds," Derby, 1844, and reprinted in *The Englishman's Magazine*, 1843, also in *Days and Seasons ; or, Church Poetry for the Year* (Derby : Henry Mozley & Sons. 1844, p. 185). The pamphlet form is the most satisfactory. In later issues (as is the case with most of Mr. Hawker's effusions), the characteristic use of capital letters, &c., has been curtailed by the printer.

ECHOES | FROM | OLD CORNWALL. | BY THE | REVEREND R. S. HAWKER, M.A., | 𝖁𝖎𝖈𝖆𝖗 𝖔𝖋 𝕸𝖔𝖗𝖜𝖊𝖓𝖘𝖙𝖔𝖜. | LONDON : | JOSEPH MASTERS, ALDERSGATE STREET. | MDCCCXLVI. | Red cloth, lettered on side, ECHOES | FROM | OLD CORNWALL. | (*Collation copy*, Miss Hawker's).

COLLATION:—Pp. viii. 98; or, A = 4 leaves, B to F 2 in twelves, the last leaf advertises "Rural Synods. The Field of Rephidim, by the same Author"; followed by Masters' Catalogue of pp. 8. Dr. Brushfield's copy is bound in blue cloth, blocked to a different pattern and lettered on the side in old English type. Mr. Wallis's copy is cased in green cloth and has no lettering on the side. A letter of Mr. Hawker's, in the possession of Dr. Brushfield, refers to this volume as a book "which did not, does not, sell, but contains poetry that I think will be appreciated one day when I am gone." Dr. Lee, however, after emphasising the fact that it "was published by that indefatigable and prolific Tractarian publisher, Mr. Joseph Masters," adds: "It had a *considerable* sale!"

A Voice | FROM | THE PLACE OF S. MORWENNA IN THE ROCKY LAND, | UTTERED | To the Sisters of Mercy, | *At the Tamar Mouth;* | AND | TO LYDIA, THEIR LADY IN THE FAITH, | "WHOSE HEART THE LORD OPENED." | BY | THE VICAR OF MORWENSTOW, | A PRIEST IN THE DIOCESE OF EXETER. | — | "Then shall appear the sign of the Son of Man in Heaven." | S. Matt. xxiv. 30. | — | LONDON: | JOSEPH MASTERS, ALDERSGATE STREET. | OXFORD: J. H. PARKER. | EXETER: H. J. WALLIS. PLYMOUTH: R. LIDSTONE. | MDCCCXLIX. | Square 16mo., paper wrappers, gilt edges. (*Collation copy*, Mr. A. Wallis's.)

COLLATION:—Half-title (on the reverse is the imprint. PLYMOUTH: | Printed by Lidstone and Brendon, George Lane.") Title (on reverse, two kneeling angels). The "Voice," pp. 5 to 10. Notes pp. 3 (page 14 and the last leaf of the half sheet are blank). The pages within rustic borders.

₊ "Lydia" was Miss Sellon, of some notoriety. The poem was not reprinted in *Cornish Ballads*, but it appears in Mr. Godwin's collection. The *brochure* is of great rarity.

THE | QUEST OF THE SANGRAAL. | *CHANT THE FIRST.* | BY | R. S. HAWKER, | VICAR OF MORWENSTOW. | "The Vessel of the Pasch, Shere-Thursday night": | "The self-same Cup, wherein the faithful Wine | "Heard God, and was obedient unto Blood" | *Line* 77, &c. | Exeter: | PRINTED FOR THE AUTHOR. | MDCCCLXIV. | Sm. 4to., crimson paper boards, lettered in old English on the side: "The Quest of the Sangraal." (*Collation copy*, Dr. Brushfield's.)

COLLATION:—Title, &c. = 3 leaves. The Poem and Appendices, B to G 3, in fours (or pp. vi. + 45). One copy was printed on vellum.

⁂ The second edition was published in *Cornish Ballads*, 1869, and it was reprinted in Mr. Godwin's collection, 1884. The editor possesses the late Mr. Westwood's privately-printed Arthurian poem, "The Sword of Kingship," 4to., 1866, in which is a pencil note, "Since included in a volume of Poems entitled 'The Quest of the Sangraal,' published by Russell [Smith?] & Co., Soho Square, 1868." No traces of such a publication have, however, been as yet encountered.

THE CORNISH BALLADS | And Other Poems | OF THE | REV. R. S. HAWKER, | VICAR OF MORWENSTOW: | Including a Second Edition of "The | Quest of the Sangraal." | — | OXFORD AND LONDON: | JAMES PARKER AND CO. | 1869. | Cr. 8vo., green cloth gilt; uncut edges. (*Collation copy*, Mr. Alfred Wallis's.)

COLLATION:—Half-title, Title (within "rules"), Dedication ("To my dear little daughters, Morwenna Pauline and Rosalind Hawker, I dedicate these pages. R. S. H."). Contents:—4 leaves + B to P 4, in eights (or pp. viii. + 214 and leaf of "Errata"). Colophon:— "Printed by James Parker and Co., Crown Yard, Oxford," followed by a leaf of (3) *errata*, and two leaves of "Books lately Published by James Parker and Co."

The Second Edition, 1884, differs from the first:—(1), in correction of *errata*; (2), in the addition of a prefatory note; (3), in the addition of "A Canticle for Christmas, 1874," in place of the former leaf of *errata*; otherwise, a paginary and lineal reprint. Green cloth, lettered on back and side. (*Collation copy*, Dr. Brushfield's.)

ST. NECTAN'S KIEVE, | AND | RECORDS OF THE WESTERN SHORE, | BY | ROBERT STEPHEN HAWKER. | *The meaning of the word, Cornwall, is the Rocky Land of* | *Strangers.*—NORDEN. | — | WILLIAM GOARD, Guide to St. Nec- | tan's Kieve Cascade. | — | CAMELFORD: | PRINTED BY RICHARD WAKEFIELD, FORE STREET. | 1868. | 12mo., green paper, printed wrapper, "Price Sixpence." (*Collation copy*, Dr. Brushfield's.)

COLLATION:—Pp. 40 (last page blank). Colophon:—"R. Wakefield, Printer, &c., Camelford."

⁂ A reprint of *Records of the Western Shore*, 1832, prepared for the use of visitors to the cascade.

BIBLIOGRAPHY.

THE POETICAL WORKS OF | ROBERT STEPHEN HAWKER, | VICAR OF MORWENSTOW, CORNWALL. | NOW FIRST COLLECTED AND ARRANGED, | WITH A PREFATORY NOTICE, | BY J. G. GODWIN. [Monogram, "R. S. H."] LONDON: | C. KEGAN PAUL & CO., I PATERNOSTER SQUARE. | 1879. | Post 8vo. (*Collation copy*, Mr. A. Wallis's.)

COLLATION:—Pp. xxiii. + 351. Colophon:—CHISWICK PRESS:—CHARLES WHITTINGHAM, TOOKS COURT, | CHANCERY LANE. | An engraved portrait, with Mr. Hawker's autograph facsimile beneath, is prefixed. Blue cloth gilt, with Mr. Hawker's characteristic monogram on the side.

FOOTPRINTS | OF | FORMER MEN | IN FAR CORNWALL. | BY R. S. HAWKER, | *VICAR OF MORWENSTOW,* | AUTHOR OF "QUEST OF THE SANGRAAL, 1864": "CORNISH BALLADS," | ETC., ETC. | LONDON: | JOHN RUSSELL SMITH, | 36, SOHO SQUARE. | MDCCCLXX. | Post 8vo., blue cloth, lettered on back and side, uncut edges. (*Collation copy*, Mr. A. Wallis's.)

COLLATION:—Title, Dedication ("To my infant daughter Juliot," dated "May, 1870"). Contents:—3 leaves. Pp. 1 to 257, followed by an advertisement of *Cornish Ballads*.

*** This volume of prose is registered here because it contains "The Storm" and other pieces of verse interspersed in the narratives of which it is composed.

MISCELLANEA.

[Under this head are collected the scattered pieces contributed to various periodicals and leaflets, so far as we can trace them. Of the latter, *many* must yet remain for registration.]

"To a Faded Flower" (signed "Reuben"), *The English Chronicle*, September 8th, 1821.

"Song of the Western Men" (Anon.), *Royal Devonport Chronicle*, September 2nd, 1826.

"Warbstow Barrow," *South Devon Monthly Museum*, iii., 200. 1834.

"The Swan," *Ibid.*, iii., 214. 1834.

"The Poor Man and His Parish Church," *Englishman's Magazine*. 1843.

BIBLIOGRAPHY.

"Earl Sinclair," *Sharpe's London Magazine*, i., 95. 1845.

"A Legend of Cornwall" (by X.), *Ibid.*, ii., 81. 1846.

"Sir Ralph de Blanc-Minster," *Once a Week*, iii., 167-8. 1867.

"The Fatal Ship, *The Sun*. 1870.

In *Notes and Queries*.

"Sir Beville" (signed "Breachan"). First Series, II., 225. 1850.

"A Cornish Folk-Song." 4to Series, I., 480. 1868.

In *Willis's Current Notes*.

"Arscott of Tetcott," December, pp. 97-8. 1853.

"Baal-Zephon," April, p. 29. 1855.

"Legends of Bells." April, p. 30. *Ibid*.

"A Christ-Cross Rhyme," November, p. 86. 1855.

"The Doom-Well of St. Madron," December, p. 93. 1855.

"The Legend of Morwenstow," January, p. 7. 1856.

"American Song," May, p. 36. 1857.

LEAFLETS.

"The Legend of S. Morwenna, A D. 50." Penzance (no date.) (A 4to. sheet, with woodcuts of the Norman Font and the Morwenstow Cliffs.)

"The Fatal Ship," signed "R. S. Hawker, 1870."

"To Alfred Tennyson, Laureate, D.C.L., on his 'Idylls of the King.'" Signed, "Ben Tamar, Morwenstow, August, 1859."

"The Christmas Tree," unsigned and undated leaflet of ten four-line verses.

"A Canticle for Christmas." 1874.

"Aurora." Twenty-five copies privately printed for Rev. W. Maskell. 1873.

[Indications of the whereabouts of many of the separate poems will be found in the editorial notes scattered throughout the following pages.]

CONTENTS.

	PAGE
Forewords	vii
Memoir	ix
Bibliography	xxiii
The Dedication	xxxix
The Song of the Western Men	1
Clovelly	3
Inscription for the Waterfall at Hayne	5
Pompeii	5
Mawgan of Melhuach	14
Featherstone's Doom	15
The Silent Tower of Bottreaux	16
The Monk Rock	19
The Spell of St. Pennah	21
Down with the Church	22
The Lady of the Mount	24
The Death-Song of Harold	25
The Burial of Harold	26
The Sisters of Glen Nectan	28
Tetcott, 1831	30
An Election Song	31
Annot of Benallay	32
Dupath Well	34
The Death Race	35
Datur Hora Quieti	37
A Rapture on the Cornish Hills	38
Trebarrow	39

CONTENTS.

	PAGE
Pater vester Pascit illa	40
Death Song	40
The Sea-bird's Cry	41
Minster Church	42
Modryb Marya—Aunt Mary	46
Morwenna Statio	47
The Saintly Names	50
The Legend of S. Morwenna	51
The Vine	53
The Well of St. Morwenna	54
"I am the Resurrection and the Life!"	55
The Western Shore	56
The Exile's Text	57
Home Once More!	59
The Poor Man and his Parish Church	61
The Song of the School: St Marks, Morwenstow	65
On the Grave of a Child in Morwenstow Churchyard	66
The Tamar Spring	67
The Storm	68
The Cell by the Sea	70
Ephphatha	73
The Signals of Levi	75
The Child Jesus	79
The Wail of the Cornish Mother	80
A Welcome to Prince Albert	82
The Second Birth of the Princess Royal	84
Duty Done	87
The Token Stream of Tidna Combe	88
The Butterfly	90
Confirmation	91
"Are They Not All Ministering Spirits?"	92
The Font	93
The Nun of Carmel's Lament	93

CONTENTS.

	PAGE
The Ringers of Lancell's Tower	95
The Kiss of Judas	96
The Lost Ship: "The President"	97
The First Prince of Wales	99
The Figure-head of the "Caledonia" at her Captain's Grave	101
Queen Guennivar's Round	102
Isha Cherioth	103
A Ballad for a Cottage Wall	104
A Legend of the Hive	105
Genoveva	109
The Lady's Well	123
Words by the Waters	125
The Twain	126
The Night Cometh	127
The Dirge	128
A Thought at Matins	129
The Baptism of the Peasant and the Prince	130
The Wolf	132
Hymn for Holy Innocents' Day	133
The Well of St. John	134
The Oblation	135
Absalom's Pillar	136
A Christ-Cross Rhyme	137
One Is Not	137
A Voice from the Place of St. Morwenna	138
Notes	141
"Be of Good Cheer!"	142
Baal Zephon	142
The Doom-Well of St. Madron	145
The Cornish Boy in Italy	146
Arscott of Tetcott	147
The Legend of Saint Cecily	150
The Legend of Saint Thekla	152

CONTENTS.

	PAGE
Miriam: Star of the Sea.	155
The Bier of Mary, Mother of God	156
Lines of Dedication to the Prince of Wales	158
To Alfred Tennyson	160
Aishah Schechinah.	161
The Southern Cross	163
King Arthur's Waes-Hael	165
Sir Beville—The Gate-Song of Stowe	166
The Comet of 1861.	167
A Croon on Hennacliff	169
The Quest of the Sangraal	171
To Eva Valentine	190
To Matilda Valentine	192
"Blue Eyes Melt; Dark Eyes Burn"	193
Written in my Lady's Dante	193
To Sophie Granville Thynne	194
Ichabod.	196
Sir Ralph de Blanc-Minster of Bien-Aimé	198
A Thought suggested by Genesis xviii. 1, 3	202
A Cornish Folk-song	203
The Smuggler's Song	204
The Fatal Ship	205
Paraphrase upon the Inscription engraved on the Statue of Sir T. D. Acland, Bart.	207
On reading Lord Derby's Translation of Homer	207
The Cornish Emigrant's Song.	208
Aurora.	209
A Fragment.	210
The Carol of the Pruss	211
Impromptu Lines	212
A Canticle for Christmas, 1874	212
The Christmas Tree	213
A Doxology	215

CONTENTS.

TRANSLATIONS :—

	PAGE
The Fisher	216
To Spring	217
To Emma	218
The Alpine Hunter	219
Pompeii	221
"Lord whither goest Thou?"	222

TENDRILS BY REUBEN :—

Preface	229
Sonnet	231
The Fairy Vision	231
Home—a Fragment	242
Night	250
On Leaving Home	252
A Tribute	253
On a Wild Violet	254
Lucretia	254
Sonnet	255
On the "Pleasures of Memory"	256
The Sea—a Fragment	257
A Night Sketch	258
The Cossack's Adieu	260
The Faded Rose	261
A Remembrance	262
The Rose of the Valley	264
A Dream	264
Memory	266
Shakespeare—a Fragment	267
To Nature	268
An Inscription for an Aged Oak	271
Diana	272

	PAGE
To Ama	273
An Epitaph on a Young Lady (from the French)	273
What Lovest Thou?	274
Introductory and Farewell Addresses	275
"The Axe is laid at the Root of the Tree"	277
David's Lament	279
"Is Nature come to this?"	280
Deborah's Song	280
Translation of an Epitaph on Rosa, Countess of Warwick	282
The Inscription over the Porch Door of Morwenstow Vicarage	283

THE DEDICATION.

TO CHARLOTTE.

Songs of the former men! the lowly rhyme
Breath'd in meek numbers by our Tamar-side;
Ye towers which rise around me, gray with time!
Ye heaving waves whereby my visions glide!
People this page with thoughts that may abide—
Beneath some living eye when I am gone,
When men shall turn the waving grass aside,
Men of strange garb perchance, and alter'd tone,
And ask whose name is worn from out that ancient stone!

What is my wish? Not that an echoing crowd
Publish my praises on some distant strand;
Not that the voices of those men be loud
With whom a strange and nameless man I stand:
'Tis the fond vision that some Western hand
Will turn this page—a native lip proclaim
Him who lov'd well and long the Rocky Land.
   Hills of Old Cornwall! in your antique fame,
    Oh! that a voice unborn might blend my future name!

THE DEDICATION.

And Thou! whose ear hath listen'd to my song,
Link'd to the minstrel by a holy tie:
Thou! to whom grateful memories belong,
Of gentle heart, kind hand, and loving eye;
For Thee I weave these words—if one should sigh
O'er him who in these vallies lov'd and died;
If a recording word be breathed hereby,
Thou shalt with him that homage still divide,
When our warm hearts be hush'd, and withering side by
  side.

1832.

[This Dedication is prefixed to *Records of the Western Shore*. The lady was Mr. Hawker's first wife, Charlotte Eliza I'Ans, to whom he was married in November, 1823. She was one of the daughters of Colonel Wrey I'Ans, of Whitstow House, near Bude Haven, Cornwall, and died February 2nd, 1863, being upwards of eighty years of age.—ED.]

POEMS.

THE SONG OF THE WESTERN MEN.

This song was first printed in a local newspaper—*The Royal Devonport Telegraph and Plymouth Chronicle*—dated September 2, 1826, without any indication of authorship. In 1827, it was published in *The Gentleman's Magazine* (XCVII., ii., 409) as a contribution from Davies Gilbert, President of the Royal Society. The ownership of the ballad was first claimed by Mr. Hawker in *Records of the Western Shore*, 1832, pp. 54—6, from which the above text, varying in some respects from the later editions, is reprinted *verb. et lit.* It has been the subject of much literary controversy, in which the late J. Eglinton Bailey, Dr. Brushfield, and others have upheld Mr. Hawker's claim to originality against the counter-assertions of less competent authorities. It was set to music by Miss Louisa T. Care in 1876.—ED.

THE SONG OF THE WESTERN MEN.

When Sir Jonathan Trelawney, one of the Seven Bishops, was committed to the Tower, the Cornish men rose, one and all, and marched as far as Exeter in their way to extort his liberation.

I.

A GOOD sword and a trusty hand!
    A merry heart and true!
King James's men shall understand
    What Cornish lads can do!

II.

And have they fix'd the where and when?
    And shall Trelawny die?
Here's twenty thousand Cornish men
    Will see the reason why!

III.

Out spake their Captain brave and bold,
    A merry wight was he:
"If London Tower were Michael's hold,
    "We'll set Trelawny free!"

IV.

"We'll cross the Tamar, land to land,
    The Severn is no stay—
All side by side, and hand to hand,
    And who shall bid us nay?

V.

"And when we come to London Wall,
  A pleasant sight to view,
Come forth! Come forth, ye Cowards all,
  To better men than you!

VI.

"Trelawny he's in keep and hold,
  Trelawny he may die;
But here's twenty thousand Cornish bold,
  Will see the reason why!"

NOTE.

With the exception of the chorus contained in the last two lines this song was written by me in 1825. It was soon after inserted in a Plymouth paper. It happened to fall into the hands of Davies Gilbert, Esq., who did me the honour to reprint it at his private press at East Bourne, under the impression, I believe, that it was the original ballad. I publish it here merely to state that it is an early composition of my own. The two lines above mentioned formed, I believe, the burthen of the old song, and are all that I can recover.

[In a later revision made for *The Cornish Ballads*, 1869, and reprinted by Mr. Godwin, Mr. Hawker's note stands as under,[1] and the refrain is altered to—

"Here's twenty thousand Cornish men
  Will know the reason why."

Also the third line in Stanza IV. is printed—

"With 'one and all,' and hand in hand."

The fourth line in Stanza V. is—

"Here's men as good as you!"

And in Stanza VI.—

"Will know the reason why!" —ED.]

---

[1] "With the exception of the choral lines,

'And shall Trelawny die?
Here's twenty thousand Cornish men
  Will know the reason why!'

and which have been, ever since the imprisonment by James the Second of the seven bishops—one of them Sir Jonathan Trelawny—a popular proverb throughout Cornwall, the whole of this song was

CLOVELLY.

'TIS eve! 'tis glimmering eve! how fair the scene,
    Touched by the soft hues of the dreamy west!
Dim hills afar, and happy vales between,
    With the tall corn's deep furrow calmly blest:
Beneath, the sea, by eve's fond gale carest,
    'Mid groves of living green that fringe its side;
Dark sails that gleam on Ocean's heaving breast
    From the glad fisher-barks that homeward glide,
    To make Clovelly's shores at pleasant evening-tide.

Hearken! the mingling sounds of earth and sea,
    The pastoral music of the bleating flock,
Blent with the sea-birds uncouth melody,
    The waves' deep murmur to the unheeding rock,
And ever and anon the impatient shock

    Of some strong billow on the sounding shore:
And hark! the rowers' deep and well-known stroke.
    Glad hearts are there, and joyful hands once more
    Furrow the whitening wave with their returning oar.

---

composed by me in the year 1825. I wrote it under a stag-horned oak in Sir Beville's Walk in Stowe Wood. It was sent by me anonymously to a Plymouth paper, and there it attracted the notice of Mr. Davies Gilbert, who reprinted it at his private press at Eastbourne under the avowed impression that it was the original ballad. It had the good fortune to win the eulogy of Sir Walter Scott, who also deemed it to be the ancient song. It was praised under the same persuasion by Lord Macaulay and by Mr. Dickens, who inserted it at first as of genuine antiquity in his *Household Words*, but who afterwards acknowledged its actual paternity in the same publication."

But turn where Art with votive hand hath twined
   A living wreath for Nature's grateful brow,
Where the lone wanderer's raptur'd footsteps wind
   'Mid rock, and glancing stream, and shadowy bough
Where scarce the valley's leafy depths allow
   The intruding sunbeam in their shade to dwell,
There doth the seamaid breathe her human vow—
   So village maidens in their envy tell—
Won from her dark blue home by that alluring dell.

A softer beauty floats along the sky,
   The moonbeam dwells upon the voiceless wave;
Far off, the night-winds steal away and die,
   Or sleep in music in their ocean-cave:
Tall oaks, whose strength the Giant Storm might brave,
   Bend in rude fondness o'er the silvery sea;
Nor can yon mountain raun[1] forbear to lave
   Her blushing clusters where the waters be,
   Murmuring around her home such touching melody.

Thou quaint Clovelly! in thy shades of rest,
   When timid Spring her pleasant task hath sped,
Or Summer pours from her redundant breast
   All fruits and flowers along thy valley's bed:
Yes! and when Autumn's golden glories spread,
   Till we forget near Winter's withering rage,
What fairer path shall woo the wanderer's tread,
   Soothe wearied hope and worn regret assuage?
   Lo! for firm youth a bower—a home for lapsing age,
    1825.

[1] The rowan tree or mountain ash.
[First printed in *Records of the Western Shore*, 1832, with some verbal differences.]

INSCRIPTION FOR THE WATERFALL AT HAYNE.

DEDICATED TO LORD BYRON.

BREATHE to the leafy woods the spell of fame,
   And teach the murmuring waters Byron's name.
So shall the soft wings of the coming breeze
People with glowing forms the cloistered trees;
And o'er yon wave beneath the willow shine
The scenes of Leman and the hues of Rhine.

1827.

POMPEII.

HOW fair the scene! the sunny smiles of day
   Flash o'er the wave in glad Sorrento's bay;
Far, far along mild Sarno's glancing stream,
The fruits and flowers of golden summer beam,
And cheer, with bright'ning hues, the lonely gloom,
That shrouds yon silent City of the Tomb!
Yes, sad Pompeii! Time's deep shadows fall
On every ruin'd arch and broken wall;
But Nature smiles as in thy happiest hour,
And decks thy lowly rest with many a flower.
Around, above, in blended beauty shine
The graceful poplar and the clasping vine;

Still the young violet,[1] in her chalice blue,
Bears to the lip of Morn her votive dew;
Still the green laurel springs to life the while,
Beneath her own Apollo's golden smile;
And o'er thy fallen beauties beams on high
The glory of the heavens—Italia's sky!

How fair the scene! e'en now to Fancy's gaze
Return the shadowy forms of other days:
Those halls, of old with mirth and music rife,
Those echoing streets that teem'd with joyous life,
The stately towers that look'd along the plain,
And the light barks that swept yon silvery main.
And see! they meet beneath the chestnut shades,
Pompeii's joyous sons and graceful maids,
Weave the light dance—the rosy chaplet twine,
Or snatch the cluster from the weary vine;
Nor think that Death can haunt so fair a scene,
The Heavens' deep blue, the Earth's unsullied green.

Devoted City! could not aught avail
When the dark omen[2] told thy fearful tale?
The giant phantom dimly seen to glide,
And the loud voice[3] that shook the mountain-side,

---

[1] The violets of this district are proverbial for their abundance and beauty.

[2] Dio Cassius, lxvi., relates, that previously to the destruction of the city, figures of gigantic size were seen hovering in the air, and that a voice like the sound of a trumpet was often heard. Probably the imagination of the inhabitants invested with human figure the vapours that preceded the eruption.

[3]   "Vox quoque per lucos vulgo exaudita silentes
      Ingens; et simulacra modis pallentia miris
      Visa sub obscurum noctis."—VIRG. *Georg.* i. 476.

With warning tones that bade thy children roam,
To seek in happier climes a calmer home?
In vain! they will not break the fatal rest
That woos them to the mountain's treacherous breast:
Fond memory blends with every mossy stone
Some early joy, some tale of pleasure flown;
And they must die where those around will weep,
And sleep for ever where their fathers sleep.
Yes! they must die: behold! yon gathering gloom
Brings on the fearful silence of the tomb;
Along Campania's sky yon murky cloud
Spreads its dark form—a City's funeral shroud.

   How brightly rose Pompeii's latest day![4]
The sun, unclouded, held his golden way;
Vineyards, in autumn's purple glories drest,
Slept in soft beauty on the mountain's breast;
The gale that wanton'd round his crested brow,
Shook living fragrance from the blossom'd bough;
And many a laughing mead and silvery stream
Drank the deep lustre of the noonday beam:
Then echoing Music rang, and Mirth grew loud
In the glad voices of the festal crowd;
The opening Theatre's[5] wide gates invite,

---

[4] Pompeii was destroyed on the 23rd of August, A.D. 79. *See* Plinii Epist. 1, vi. 16, 20; Dio Cassius, lxvi. It remained undiscovered during fifteen centuries.

[5] Eustace and other modern writers have thought it improbable that the inhabitants of Pompeii could have assembled to enjoy the amusement of the theatre after the shocks of the earthquake and other symptoms of danger which preceded the eruption; but as their theatrical representations partook of the nature of religious solemnities, there does not seem sufficient reason to disregard the positive assertion of Dio Cassius to the contrary.

The choral dance is there, the solemn rite—
There breathes the immortal Muse her spell around,
And swelling thousands flood the fated ground.
See! where arise before th' enraptur'd throng,
The fabled scenes, the shadowy forms of Song!
Gods, that with heroes leave their starry bowers,
Their fragrant hair entwin'd with radiant flowers,
Haunt the dim grove, beside the fountain dwell—
Strike the deep lyre, or sound the wreathèd shell—
With forms of heavenly mould, but hearts that glow
With human passion, melt with human woe:
Breathless they gaze, while white-robed priests advance,
And graceful virgins lead the sacred dance;
They listen, mute, while mingling tones prolong
The lofty accent, and the pealing song,
Echo th' unbending Titan's haughty groan,
Or in the Colchian's woes forgot their own![6]
Why feels each throbbing heart that shuddering chill?
The Music falters, and the Dance is still—
" Is it pale twilight stealing o'er the plain?
" Or starless eve that holds unwonted reign?"
Hark to the thrilling answer! Who shall tell
When thick and fast th' unsparing tempest fell,
And stern Vesuvius pour'd along the vale
His molten cataracts, and his burning hail?
Oh! who shall paint, in that o'erwhelming hour,
Death's varying forms, and Horror's withering power?

[6] Ivory tickets of admission were found in the vicinity of one of the theatres, inscribed on one side with the name of a play of Æschylus, and on the other with a representation of the theatre itself. One or two of these are preserved in the studio at Naples.

Earthquake! wild Earthquake! rends that heaving plain,
Cleaves the firm rock, and swells the beetling main:
Here, yawns the ready grave, and, raging, leap
Earth's secret fountains from their troubled sleep;
There, from the quivering mountain bursts on high
The pillar'd flame that wars along the sky!
On, on they press, and maddening seek in vain
Some soothing refuge from the fiery rain—
Their home? it can but yield a living tomb!
Round the lov'd hearth is brooding deepest gloom.
Yon sea? its angry surges scorching rave,
And death-fires gleam upon the ruddy wave!
Oh! for one breath of that reviving gale,
That swept at dewy morn along the vale!
For one sad glance of their beloved sky,
To soothe, though vain, their parting agony!
Yon mother bows in vain her shuddering form,
Her babe to shield from that relentless storm:
Cold are those limbs her clasping arms constrain,
Even the soft shelter of her breast is vain!
Gaze on that form! 'tis Beauty's softest maid,
The rose's rival in her native shade—
For her had Pleasure reared her fairest bowers,
And Song and Dance had sped the laughing hours:
See! o'er her brow the kindling ashes glow,
And the red shower o'erwhelms her breast of snow;
She seeks that loved one—never false till then—
She calls on him—who answers not again:
Loose o'er her bosom flames her golden hair,
And every thrilling accent breathes despair!

Even the stern priest, who saw with raptur'd view
The deathless forms of Heaven's ethereal blue,
Who drank, with glowing ear, the mystic tone,
That clothed his lips with wonders not their own,
Beheld the immortal marble frown in vain,
And fires triumphant grasp the sacred fane,
Forsook at last the unavailing shrine,
And cursed his faithless gods—no more divine!

   Morn came in beauty still—and shone as fair,
Though cold the hearts that hail'd its radiance there,
And Evening, crown'd with many a starry gem,
Sent down her softest smile—though not for them!
Where gleam'd afar Pompeii's graceful towers,
Where hill and vale were cloth'd with vintage bowers,
O'er a dark waste the smouldering ashes spread,
A pall above the dying and the dead.

   Still the dim city slept in safest shade,
Though the wild waves another Queen obeyed,
And sad Italia, on her angry shore,
Beheld the North its ruthless myriads pour;
And nature scattered all her treasures round,
And graced with fairest hues the blighted ground.
There oft, at glowing noon, the village maid
Sought the deep shelter of the vineyard shade;
Beheld the olive bud—the wild-flower wave,
Nor knew her step was on a people's grave!
But see! once more beneath the smiles of day,
The dreary mist of ages melts away!
Again Pompeii, 'mid the brightening gloom,
Comes forth in beauty from her lonely tomb.
Lovely in ruin—graceful in decay,

The silent City rears her walls of grey:
The clasping ivy hangs her faithful shade,
As if to hide the wreck that time had made;
The shattered column on the lonely ground
Is glittering still, with fresh acanthus crowned;
And where her Parian rival moulders near,
The drooping lily pours her softest tear!
How sadly sweet with pensive step to roam
Amid the ruin'd wall, the tottering dome!
The path just worn by human feet is here,
Their echoes almost reach the listening ear;
The marble halls with rich mosaic drest;
The portal wide that woos the lingering guest;
Altars, with fresh and living chaplets crown'd,
From those wild flowers that spring fantastic round;
The unfinish'd painting, and the pallet nigh,
Whose added hues must fairer charms supply—
These mingle here, until th' unconscious feet
Roam on, intent some gathering crowd to meet;
And cheated Fancy, in her dreamy mood,
Will half forget that it is solitude!

   Yes, all is solitude! fear not to tread,
Through gates unwatch'd, the City of the Dead!
Explore with pausing step th' unpeopled path,
View the proud hall—survey the stately bath,
Where swelling roofs their noblest shelter raise;
Enter! no voice shall check th' intruder's gaze!
See! the dread legion's peaceful home is here,
The signs of martial life are scattered near.
Yon helm, unclasp'd to ease some Warrior's brow,
The sword his weary arm resign'd but now,

Th' unfinish'd sentence traced along the wall,
Broke by the hoarse Centurion's startling call:
Hark! did their sounding tramp re-echo round?
Or breath'd the hollow gale that fancied sound?
Behold! where 'mid yon fane, so long divine,
Sad Isis mourns her desolated shrine!
Will none the mellow reed's soft music breathe?
Or twine from yonder flowers the victim's wreath?
None to yon altar lead with suppliant strain
The milk-white monarch of the herd again?[7]
All, all is mute! save sadly answering nigh
The night-bird's shriek, the shrill cicada's cry.
Yet may you trace along the furrow'd street,
The chariot's track—the print of frequent feet;
The gate unclosed, as if by recent hand;
The hearth, where yet the guardian Lares stand;
Still on the walls the words of welcome shine,[8]
And ready vases proffer joyous wine:[9]
But where the hum of men? the sounds of life?
The Temple's pageant, and the Forum's strife?
The forms and voices, such as should belong
To that bright clime, the land of Love and Song?
How sadly echoing to the stranger's tread,
These walls respond, like voices from the dead!
And sadder traces—darker scenes are there,
Tales of the Tomb, and records of Despair;

[7] "Hinc albi Clitumne greges et maxima taurus Victima."—VIRG. *Georg.* ii. 146.

[8] On many of the walls the word, *Salve,* is carved over the door.

[9] "The amphoræ which contained wine still remain, and the marble slabs are marked with cups and glasses."—EUSTACE.

In Death's chill grasp unconscious arms enfold
The fatal burden of their cherished gold. [10]
Here, wasted relics, as in mockery, dwell
Beside some treasure loved in life too well;
There, faithful hearts have moulder'd side by side,
And hands are claspt that Death could not divide!
None, none shall tell that hour of fearful strife,
When Death must share the consciousness of Life;
When sullen Famine, slow Despair consume
The living tenants of the massive tomb;
Long could they hear, above th' incumbent plain,
The music of the breeze awake again,
The waves' deep echo on the distant shore,
And murmuring streams, that they should see no more!
Away! dread scene! and o'er the harrowing view
Let Night's dim shadows fling their darkest hue!
 But there, if still beneath some nameless stone,
By waving weeds and ivy-wreaths o'ergrown,
Lurk the grey spoils of Poet or of Sage,
Tully's deep lore, or Livy's pictured page.
If sweet Menander, where his relics fade,
Mourn the dark refuge of Oblivion's shade;
Oh! may their treasures burst the darkling mine;
Glow in the living voice, the breathing line;
Their vestal fire our midnight lamp illume,
And kindle Learning's torch from sad Pompeii's tomb!

---

[10] At the door of the court of one of the houses skeletons were found, one with a key, another with a purse."—EUSTACE.

MAWGAN OF MELHUACH.

'TWAS a fierce night when old Mawgan died,
   Men shuddered to hear the rolling tide:
The wreckers fled fast from the awful shore,
They had heard strange voices amid the roar.

" Out with the boat there," some one cried,—
" Will he never come? we shall lose the tide:
His berth is trim and his cabin stored,
He's a weary long time coming on board."

The old man struggled upon the bed:
He knew the words that the voices said;
Wildly he shriek'd as his eyes grew dim,
" He was dead! he was dead! when I buried him."

Hark yet again to the devilish roar!
" He was nimbler once with a ship on shore;
" Come! come! old man, 'tis a vain delay,
" We must make the offing by break of day."

Hard was the struggle, but at the last,
With a stormy pang old Mawgan pass'd,
And away, away, beneath their sight,
Gleam'd the red sail at pitch of night.

NOTE.

Gilbert Mawgan, a noted wrecker, lived in a hut that stood by the sea shore at Mellhuach, or The Vale of the Lark. Among other crimes it is said that he once buried the captain of a vessel, whom he found exhausted on the strand, alive! At the death of the old man, they told me that a vessel came up the Channel, made for Mellhuach bay and lay-to amid a tremendous surf. When Mawgan ceased to breathe she stood-out to sea and disappeared.

[First printed in *Records of the Western Shore*, 1832. The above note was omitted by Mr. Godwin, who states that the poem was published in *Once a Week*, Oct. 30, 1831, a manifest error.—ED.]

FEATHERSTONE'S DOOM.

TWIST thou and twine! in light and gloom
    A spell is on thine hand;
The wind shall be thy changeful loom,
    Thy web the shifting sand.

Twine from this hour, in ceaseless toil,
    On Blackrock's[1] sullen shore;
Till cordage of the sand shall coil
    Where crested surges roar.

'Tis for that hour, when, from the wave,
    Near voices wildly cried;
When thy stern hand no succour gave,
    The cable at thy side.

Twist thou and twine! in light and gloom
    The spell is on thine hand;
The wind shall be thy changeful loom,
    Thy web the shifting sand.

1831.

[1] The Blackrock is a bold, dark, pillared mass of schist, which rises midway on the shore of Widemouth Bay, near Bude, and is held to be the lair of the troubled spirit of Featherstone the wrecker, imprisoned therein until he shall have accomplished his doom.

[First printed in *Records of the Western Shore*, 1831.]

THE SILENT TOWER OF BOTTREAUX.

TINTADGEL[1] bells ring o'er the tide,
　　The boy leans on his vessel's side ;
He hears that sound, and dreams of home
Soothe the wild orphan of the foam.
　　" Come to thy God in time ! "
　　Thus saith their pealing chime :
　　" Youth, manhood, old age past,
　　" Come to thy God at last."

But why are Bottreaux' echoes still ?
Her Tower stands proudly on the hill ;
Yet the strange chough^e that home hath found,
The lamb lies sleeping on the ground.
　　" Come to thy God in time ! "
　　Should be her answering chime :
　　" Come to thy God at last ! "
　　Should echo on the blast.

The ship rode down with courses free,
The daughter of a distant sea :

---

[1] The rugged heights that line the seashore in the neighbourhood of Tintadgel Castle and Church are crested with towers. Among these, that of Bottreaux, or, as it is now written, Boscastle, is without bells. The silence of this wild and lonely churchyard on festive or solemn occasions is not a little striking. On inquiry I was told that the bells were once shipped for this church, but that when the vessel was within sight of the tower the blasphemy of her captain was punished in the manner related in the Poem. The bells, they told me, still lie in the bay, and announce by strange sounds the approach of a storm.

Her sheet was loose, her anchor stored,
The merry Bottreaux bells[3] on board.
 " Come to thy God in time ! "
 Rung out Tintadgel chime;
 " Youth, manhood, old age past,
 " Come to thy God at last ! "

The pilot heard his native bells
Hang on the breeze in fitful swells;
" Thank God ! " with reverent brow he cried,
" We'll make the shore with evening's tide."
 " Come to thy God in time ! "
 It was his marriage chime :
 " Youth, manhood, old age past,"
 His bell must ring at last.

" Thank God, thou whining knave ! on land,
" But thank, at sea, the steersman's hand,"
" The captain's voice above the gale—
" Thank the good ship and ready sail,"
 " Come to thy God in time ! "
 Sad grew the boding chime :
 " Come to thy God at last ! "
 Boom'd heavy on the blast.

Uprose that sea ! as if it heard
The mighty Master's signal-word :

[2] This wild bird chiefly haunts the coasts of Devon and Cornwall. The common people believe that the soul of King Arthur inhabits one of these birds, and no entreaty or bribe would induce an old Tintadgel quarry-man to kill me one.

[3] The castle mound of the former residence of the Barons of Bottreaux is the sole relic of their race.

What thrills the captain's whitening lip?
The death-groans of his sinking ship.
 "Come to thy God in time!"
 Swung deep the funeral chime:
 "Grace, mercy, kindness past,
 "Come to thy God at last!"

Long did the rescued pilot tell—
When grey hairs o'er his forehead fell,
While those around would hear and weep—
That fearful judgment of the deep,
 "Come to thy God in time!"
 He read his native chime:
 "Youth, manhood, old age past,"
 His bell rang out at last.

Still when the storm of Bottreaux' waves
Is wakening in his weedy caves:
Those bells, that sullen surges hide,
Peal their deep notes beneath the tide:
 "Come to thy God in time!"
 Thus saith the ocean chime:
 "Storm, billow, whirlwind past,
 "Come to thy God at last!"

1831.

[First published in *Records of the Western Shore*, 1832.]

THE MONK ROCK.

YOU have heard of the Holy Well, my love,
   On Cuthbert's [1] storied ground,
The cloister'd cave all dark above,
   The cold waves moaning round.

A pillar'd rock frowns stately there,
   Far o'er the baffled wave;
" The Monk " is the ancient name it bare
   Which our Cornish fathers gave.

. . . . .

The moon was cold on the furrow'd sand
   Without that rocky shade,
When the print of Crantock's burning hand,[2]
   On the maiden's brow was laid—

'Tis not to pray—'tis not to shrive—
   Therefore what doth she there?
" She loved," is the answer the legends give,
   " She loved too well to fear."

" Now Saint Cuthbert aid!" was the cry they heard,
   That deep and distant tone;
'Twas not the voice of the ocean bird
   'Twas not the sea-maid's moan.

[1] *On Cuthbert's Storied Ground.*] Cuthbert is pronounced, and sometimes written, *Cubert*.

[2] *When the print of Crantock's burning hand.*] The Collegiate Church of Saint Crantock, or Carantock, consisted of a Dean and nine Prebendaries. It was conveyed to the Church of Exeter in the year 1236. The college was dissolved in 1534.

They found her not at break of morn,
  The dark friar was not there,
Another priest for his cell is shorn—
  Her hearth hath a vacant chair.

. . . . .

A fountain leaps to gushing life
  In that unwonted spot;
The surges war, in fruitless strife,
  With a rock that heedeth not.

Plunge those you love in that Sacred Well
  At moonlight's mystic hour—
They say that sin shall pass therein,
  The Fiend will lose his power.

But shun that Rock amid the Sea!
  Its cold depths darkly bear
A breast all quick with agony,
  Hot with the old despair.

In an antique book these things are told,
  Tales of a former age;
And shapes uncouth, in hues of gold,
  Are graven on the page.

You have heard of the Holy Well, my love,
  On Cuthbert's storied ground;
The cloister'd cave all dark above
  The cold waves moaning round.

[From *Records of the Western Shore*, 1832—not included in Mr. Godwin's collection.—ED.]

THE SPELL OF ST. PENNAH.

"Daughter, my daughter! it is the time;
  The bell hath swung with the midnight chime.
" By thy lost soul and thy tarnished fame,
" Bring me thy lover's unuttered name!"

" Mother, my mother! how can I brook
" From his awful eye the withering look?
" How can I brave that boding tone—
"' Death to our love when my name is known?'"

" Sign thou the Cross on his bended brow;
" Breathe in his ear Saint Pennah's vow;
" Free thy poor soul from her sinful load—
" False to thy lover, but true to thy God!"

She hath made that Sign in her fond despair;
She hath breathed in fierce love Saint Pennah's prayer;
She hath lightened her soul of its sinful load—
False to her lover, but true to her God.

. . . . .

It was a Spirit that turned to the sky
Th' immortal grief of his sullen eye;
And sad was the wild farewell he gave,
As the deep voice of a sounding wave.

" Home! Home, once more, to my woful toil!
" Back to our den, to gibber and coil,
" Where the gliding shadows mourn for rest,
" Each with his hand on his weary breast!"

Now this same Saint Pennah, you understand,
Was the frailest flower of the Rocky Land;[1]
Hard penance she did for crimes unshriven,
Till the sinner on earth was a saint in heaven.

She framed in her death this touching spell,
Which the daughter said who had loved too well—
Thus was lightened her soul of its weary load,
And the sinner was gathered unto God!

[1] Cornwall.

Nov. 15th, 1831.

[From *Records of the Western Shore*, 1832—not included in Mr. Godwin's collection.—ED.]

"DOWN WITH THE CHURCH."

AN ELECTIONEERING CRY.

An electioneering song, written when Sir R. Vyvyan and Sir C. Lemon were standing for East Cornwall.

SHALL the grey tower in ruin spread?
   And must the furrow hold your dead?
Our best-belovèd are at rest,
Their cold hands folded on their breast,—
Spring's placid flowers their ashes hide,
And we shall slumber at their side.

Shall the grey tower in ruin bow?
Must the babe die with nameless brow?

Or common hands in mockery fling
The unbless'd waters of the spring?
Where will the dove-like spirit rest
When yon old Church shall close her breast?

Shall the grey tower in silence stand
When the heart thrills within the hand,
And beauty's lip to youth hath given
The vow on Earth that links for Heaven?
Shall no glad peal from churchyard grey
Cheer the young matron's homeward way?

Yes! by the heart of England's pride
Still beating on the mountain side!
Yes! by the spirit of former men,
That slumbers in each Cornish glen!
The cry of triumph yet shall ring—
The Vyvyan-cry—"Our Church and King!"

Fair dame! the babe that climbs thy knee
Would lift its lisping voice to thee.
Maiden! with fond one at thy side—
Tell! by the holy name of Bride!
Mourner! by that beneath the pall!—
Shall the grey tower in ruin fall?

No! though the sweat of faction reek
On each reformer's clammy cheek,
No! though the voice of discord rend
The stately towers that none shall bend,
No! while the Cornish cry can ring—
The Vyvyan-cry—"Our Church and King!"

May 2nd, 1831.

THE LADY OF THE MOUNT.

*"To live in hearts we leave behind,
Is not to die."*

A LONELY lady mourns upon the land
    Where Mount St. Michael[1] guards the Atlantic
    wave;
A pale brow drooping on a wasted hand,—
The Lady Katherine Gordon[2]—she who gave
All that a bard could hymn or warrior crave
To Warbeck, vaunted heir of York's true line.
She loved him well in life, and o'er his grave,
Hear it, ye misbelievers! as a shrine
She breath'd into his soul a passion all divine!

Slowly she dies! and, one by one, the hues
Pass from her shining cheek, till all is pale;
Tears fall thereon—the unavailing dews
Impearl those leaves that wave beneath the gale.
Fame, worship, wealth! and what could these avail?
He for whom all were dear was far away—

---

[1] *Mount St. Michael.*] A band of monks, from a place of the same name on the Loire, founded a Priory on this rock before the time of Edward the Confessor.

[2] *The Lady Katherine Gordon.*] "She loved Warbeck," says Bacon, "utterly in all his fortunes, and the name of The White Rose, which he gave her in his pride, men continued unto her, because of her beauty." He left her at St. Michael's Mount on his march to London. Of her fate after his capture and death, there are conflicting legends. Our Cornish dames assert that she died—their husbands, that she married again. I have adopted the more poetical catastrophe.

Yet the proud name he gave shall none assail,
Our bards still call'd her, in their honouring lay,
The White Rose of Old England, unto her dying day.

The White Rose of Old England! at that name
Our hearts shall burn within us. Tales they tell
Of a grey band of monks that seaward came
From the rich Loire; and where these surges swell
They rear'd, in memory of their native cell,
Walls, where St. Michael still might honour'd be.
At the Eighth Harry's breath their cloister fell:—
Therefore the storied rock and girdling sea,
Thou Lady of the Dead! we consecrate to thee!

1832

[First printed in *Records of the Western Shore*, 1832.]

THE DEATH-SONG OF HAROLD,

Surnamed the Red,

Slain at the Battle of Camlan.

TELL my mother, Swanha, upon Norroway's dear shore,
She will comb the yellow hair of her eldest-born no more;
And tell the maiden Githa, which should have been my bride,
Thou sawest me kiss this token, it was with me when I died.

Bid Hacho fill the mead-bowl, beside my vacant chair,
And raise a Runic chorus, for him who is not there;
And when they urge the wolf-hound, upon the failing
    prey,
Charge Ailric that he blow one blast, for the hunter
    far away.

They came, the shadowy sisters, they stood beside
    my bed,
They spake of me last night, and I heard the words
    they said;
" Why doth Red Harold loiter? Again must Odin
    say,
We tarry for an absent guest, the Fame of Norro-
    way!"

1832.

THE BURIAL OF HAROLD.

STERN Harold hath stiffened beneath his tall
    shield,
For the Normans have slain him on Hastings' red
    field;
And William hath sworn in the hour of his pride,
That the raven shall rend him e'en there as he died.

Ten marks of red gold, Canon Osgod hath paid
For suff'rance to bury the bones of the dead;
And the hawk from his wrist Ailric Forester gave,
To win for the Lord of his childhood a grave.

"Away with your dead!" cried the Bastard at last,
So on to the red field of battle they pass'd;
But in vain by the heaps Canon Osgod went by,
And vain the keen glance of the Falconer's eye.

"Bring Edith!" they said (whom the bard in his theme,
Once named to proud Harold, "the Swan of the Stream)."
She came, and they found her bent low at his side—
Could Death hide the warrior from Edith, his bride?

"Now, the Canon to Mass and the Hunter to horn!"
She shrieked in her anguish and laughed in her scorn—
"See the hand! the red hand that long pillowed my rest!
And the brow, the cold brow, that lay warm on my breast!"

1832.

This poem was suggested by the following romantic story, told by the author of the Waltham MS. in the Cottonian Library. . .
"If we may believe him, two of the Canons, Osgod Cnoppe and Ailric, the childe-maister, were sent to be spectators of the battle. They obtained from William, to whom they presented ten marks of gold, permission to search for the body of their benefactor. Unable to distinguish it among the heaps of the slain, they sent for Harold's mistress, Editha, surnamed *The Fair* and *The Swan's Neck*. By her his features were recognised. The corpse was interred at Waltham with regal honours in the presence of several Norman earls and gentlemen."—LINGARD'S *History of England.*

[This poem is here, for the first time, printed from a MS. in Mr. Hawker's handwriting. It differs materially from the version given in *Records of the Western Shore*, first edition, 1832, which omits the last verse and has no explanatory note. It was excluded by Mr. Godwin from his collection of Mr. Hawker's " Poetical Works."
—ED.]

THE SISTERS OF GLEN NECTAN.

IT is from Nectan's[1] mossy steep,
    The foamy waters flash and leap:
It is where shrinking wild-flowers grow,
They lave the nymph that dwells below.

But wherefore in this far-off dell,
The reliques of a human cell?
Where the sad stream and lonely wind
Bring man no tidings of his kind.

"Long years agone," the old man said,
'Twas told him by his grandsire dead:
"One day two ancient sisters came:
None there could tell their race or name;

---

[1] In a rocky gorge, midway between the castles of Bottreaux and Dundagel, there is a fall of waters into a hollow cauldron of native stone, which has borne for ten centuries the name of St. Nectan's Kieve. He was the brother of St. Morwenna, and like her is one of the storied names along this northern shore. He founded the Stations, now the Churches, of Hartland and Wellcombe; and bequeathed his name to other sacred places by the "Severn Sea," in the former ages of Cornish faith.

When I first visited his Kieve, in 1830, the outline of an oratory, or the reliques of a cell, stood by the brook, on a knoll, just where the waters took their leap. There is a local legend linked with this ruined abode, which was told me on the spot; and which I expanded at the time into the above ballad. I have recognized the coinage of my brain in the prosaic paraphrases of Wilkie Collins, Walter White, and other subsequent writers; but with regard to any claimant for the original imagination, I must reply, in the language of Jack Cade, "No, no; I invented it myself."

"Their speech was not in Cornish phrase,
Their garb had signs of loftier days;
Slight food they took from hands of men,
They withered slowly in that glen.

"One died—the other's sunken eye
Gushed till the fount of tears was dry;
A wild and withering thought had she,
' I shall have none to weep for me.'

"They found her silent at the last,
Bent in the shape wherein she passed;
Where her lone seat long used to stand,
Her head upon her shrivelled hand."

Did fancy give this legend birth?
The grandame's tale for winter hearth:
Or some dead bard, by Nectan's stream,
People these banks with such a dream?

We know not: but it suits the scene,
To think such wild things here have been:
What spot more meet could grief or sin
Choose, at the last, to wither in?

1832.

[First printed, as "The Sisters of the Glen," in *Records of the Western Shore*, 1832, and again as Appendix A, in the first edition of *The Quest of the Sangrael*, where it is entitled "Saint Nectan's Kieve." The original note calls the waterfall "Nathan's Kieve," and the name "Nathan" occurs in the poem in place of Nectan. However, in *Echoes from Old Cornwall*, 1846, this poem is entitled "The Sisters of Glen Neots," although the original title returns in *The Cornish Ballads*, 1870. It is also worthy of remark that in the second series of *Records*, 1836, Mr. Hawker has inserted a poem by Arthur Kelly, Esq., Sheriff of Cornwall, entitled "Nathan's Kieve.—ED.]

TETCOTT, 1831;[1]

IN WHICH YEAR SIR WILLIAM MOLESWORTH CAUSED THE OLD HOUSE TO BE TAKEN DOWN, AND A NEW ONE BUILT.

SHADE of the Hunter old! if aught could roam
From the dim cloisters of that shadowy home,
Where the far spirits of each severed clime,
The sad and placid, coil and bide their time,
If love survive, or memory endear,
Shade of the Hunter old! thou would'st be here!

Oh, for the Squire that shook at break of morn,
Dew from the trees with echo of his horn!
The gathering scene, where Arscott's lightest word
Went like a trumpet to the hearts that heard!
The dogs that knew the meaning of his voice,
From the grim fox-hound to my lady's choice.
The steed that waited till his hand carest,
And old Black John[2] that gave and bare the jest.

The good old Squire! once more along the glen,
Oh, for the scenes of old! the former men!
That hill's far echoes sped the starting cry,
Within yon vale the worn prey rushed to die.

---

[1] *Vide* also "Arscott of Tetcott," p. 147.

[2] For an account of Black John, *vide* "Footprints of Former Men in Far Cornwall," p. 67.

Yes! in these fields, beneath his stately form,
Dashed the wild steed with footsteps like the storm.

'Tis past; that ivy, last of all her race,
Yields the grey dwelling from her sad embrace.
The walls! the walls! that felt his father's breath,
Th' accustomed room he loved so well in death,
Are lowly laid—and in their place will stand
A roof unknown—a stranger in the land.

1831.

AN ELECTION SONG.

Written when Sir Salusbury Trelawny contested the county in 1832, against my impulses and judgment, but I was subdued by Lady Trelawny in her peremptory way.—R. S. H.

AND do they scorn Tre, Pol, and Pen?
    And shall Trelawny die?
Here's twenty thousand Cornish men
    Will know the reason why!

The former spirit is not fled,
    Where Cornish hearts combine,
We bow before the noble dead,
    And laud their living line!

Be chainless as yon rushing wave,
    Free as your native air;
But honour to the good and brave,
    And homage to the fair!

Think on the warrior's waving hand,
    The patriot's lasting fame,
And follow o'er the Rocky Land,
    The old Trelawny name!

Up with your hearts, Tre, Pol, and Pen!
    They bid Trelawny die:
But twenty thousand Cornish men
    Will know the reason why!

1832.

ANNOT OF BENALLAY.

AT lone midnight the death-bell tolled,
    To summon Annot's clay;
For common eyes must not behold
    The griefs of Benallay.

Meek daughter of a haughty line,
    Was Lady Annot born:
That light which was not long to shine,
    The sun that set at morn.

They shrouded her in maiden white,
    They buried her in pall;
And the ring *He* gave her faith to plight
    Shines on her finger small.

The Curate reads the deadman's prayer,
    The sullen Leech stands by:
The sob of voiceless love is there,
    And sorrow's vacant eye.

'Tis over! Two and two they tread
    The churchyard's homeward way:
Farewell! farewell! thou lovely dead:
    Thou Flower of Benallay.

The sexton stalks with tottering limb
    Along the chancel floor:
He waits, that old man grey and grim,
    To close the narrow door.

"Shame! Shame! these rings of stones and gold,"
    The ghastly caitiff said,
" Better that living hands should hold
    Than glisten on the dead."

The evil wish wrought evil deed,
    The pall is rent away:
And lo! beneath the shatter'd lid,
    The Flower of Benallay!

But life gleams from those opening eyes!
    Blood thrills that lifted hand!
And awful words are in her cries,
    Which none may understand!

Joy! 'tis the miracle of yore,
    Of the city callèd Nain:—
Lo! glad feet throng the sculptur'd floor
    To hail their dead again!

Joy in the halls of Benallay !
   A stately feast is spread ;
Lord Harold is the bridegroom gay,
   The Bride th' arisen dead.

The facts on which the above Ballad is founded are well known in Cornwall. I have only altered the name and place.

[From *Records of the Western Shore*, 1832. Printed also in *The Cornish Ballads*, with some slight verbal difference.]

DUPATH WELL.

HEAR how the noble Siward died !
   The Leech hath told the woeful bride
'Tis vain : his passing hour is nigh,
And death must quench her warrior's eye.

" Bring me," he said, " the steel I wore
When Dupath spring was dark with gore,
The spear I raised for Githa's glove,
Those trophies of my wars and love."

Upright he sate within the bed,
The helm on his unyielding head :
Sternly he lean'd upon his spear,
He knew his passing hour was near.

" Githa ! thine hand !" how wild that cry,
How fiercely glared his flashing eye ;
" Sound ! herald !" was his shout of pride :
Hear how the noble Siward died !

A roof must shade that storied stream,
Her dying lord's remember'd theme;
A daily vow that lady said
Where glory wreath'd the hero dead.

Gaze, maiden, gaze on Dupath Well,
Time yet hath spar'd that solemn cell—
In memory of old love and pride:
Hear how the noble Siward died.

March 2, 1832.

Dupath Spring gushes at the foot of Hingston Tor. Its waters flow through the arched door of a granite cell; and, like most of the guarded wells of our country, "it hath a meaning," which I have endeavoured to record. Goetz of the Iron Hand and other warriors imitated in after times the death of Siward.

[From *Records of the Western Shore*, 1832. Reprinted, omitting the above note, in *The Cornish Ballads*.]

THE DEATH-RACE.

WATCH ye, and ward ye! a ship in sight,
And bearing down for Trebarra[1] Height,
She folds her wings by that rocky strand:
Watch ye, and ward ye![2] a boat on land!

[1] *Trebarra.*] Two strangers, with their followers-at-arms, arrived on a certain night at a village near Trebarra strand. A corpse, carried on a bier and covered with a pall, seemed the chief object of their care. One of these strangers remained by the body while the other watched the sea. At dawn, a ship appeared in sight, neared the shore, and sent off a boat. The strangers hastened to the beach, placed the corpse in the boat, embarked with it and were never heard of more. This legend, a distorted account of an actual occurrence in the twelfth century, is still current in the neighbourhood of Trebarra, and was related to me there.

[2] *Watch ye, and ward ye.*] There are remains of many small buildings on this coast which the people call "Watch and Ward Towers," as they no doubt were when piracy was common on the coast, in the old times.

Hush! for they glide from yonder cave
To greet these strangers of the wave;
Wait! since they pace the seaward glen
With the measured tread of mourning men.

"Hold! masters, hold! ye tarry here,
What corpse is laid on your solemn bier?
Yon minster-ground were a calmer grave
Than the roving bark, or the weedy wave!"

"Strong vows we made to our sister dead
To hew in fair France her narrow bed;
And her angry ghost will win no rest
If your Cornish earth lie on her breast."

They rend that pall in the glaring light,
By St. Michael of Carne! 'twas an awful sight!
For those folded hands were meekly laid
On the silent breast of a shrouded maid.

"God speed, my masters, your mournful way!
Go, bury your dead where best ye may!
But the Norroway barks are over the deep,
So we watch and ward from our guarded steep."

Who comes with weapon? who comes with steed?
Ye may hear far off their clanking speed;
What knight in steel is thundering on?
Ye may know the voice of the grim Sir John.

"Saw ye my daughter, my Gwennah bright,
Borne out for dead at the deep of night?"
"Too late! too late!" cried the warder pale,
"Lo! the full deck, and the rushing sail!"

They have roused that maid from her trance of sleep,
They have spread their sails to the roaring deep;
Watch ye, and ward ye! with wind and tide,
Fitz-Walter hath won his Cornish bride.

[From *Records of the Western Shore*, 1832, where the Poem is entitled "The Corpse-Race." The notes were excluded from *The Cornish Ballads*, and from Mr. Godwin's collection.—ED.]

DATUR HORA QUIETI.

To the MS. of this Poem is the following note:—"Why do you wish the burial to be at five o'clock?" "Because it was the time at which he used to leave work."

"AT eve should be the time," they said,
   "To close their brother's narrow bed:"
'Tis at that pleasant hour of day
The labourer treads his homeward way.

His work was o'er, his toil was done,
And therefore with the set of sun,
To wait the wages of the dead,
We laid our hireling in his bed.

"So when even was come, the Lord of the Vineyard saith unto his steward, call the labourers, and give them their hire."—Saint Matthew xx. 8.

Among the rural inhabitants of Cornwall the burial of the dead usually takes place in the evening, because the bearers have then "left work."

[First printed in the Second Series of *Records of the Western Shore*, 1836, as "The Funeral Time," and by Mr. Godwin, omitting the footnotes, as "The Burial Hour." I think the Latin title was suggested by Turner's beautiful vignette upon the last page of Rogers' *Poems*, 1834.—ED.]

A RAPTURE ON THE CORNISH HILLS.

I STOOD at the foot of Rocky Carradon—
    The massive monuments of a vast religion,
Piled by the strength of unknown hands, were there
The everlasting hills, around, afar,
Uplifted their huge fronts, the natural altars
Reared by the Earth to its surrounding God.
I heard a Voice, as the sound of many waters:—
" What do'st thou here, Elijah?" And I said,
" What doth *he* here, Man that is born of woman?
The clouds may haunt these mountains; the fierce storm
Coiled in his caverned lair—that wild torrent
Leaps from a native land: but Man! O Lord!
What doth *he* here!"

            STRANGER.
Did'st thou not fear the Voice?

            THE BARD.
I could not, at the foot of Rocky Carradon.

  1832.

            NOTE.

    There is a wide extent of hilly moorland stretching from Rough Tor to Carradon and heaped with rude structures of various kinds, that would reward the researches of an Antiquary. The cromlech, piled rocks, and unhewn pillar, are commonly referred to the times of Druidical worship. To me, they seem to claim a more ancient origin. A simple structure of stone was the usual altar and monument of the Patriarchal Religion. The same feelings would actuate the heirs of that creed in Cornwall as in Palestine; and the same motives would induce them to rear a pillar there, and to pour oil thereon, and to call it the Place of God.

    [From *Records of the Western Shore*, 1832, excluded from Mr. Godwin's collection.—ED.]

TREBARROW.

DID the wild blast of battle sound,
    Of old, from yonder lonely mound?
Race of Pendragen! did ye pour
On this dear earth your votive gore?

Did stern swords cleave along this plain
The loose rank of the roving Dane?
Or Norman charger's sounding tread
Smite the meek daisy's Saxon head?

The wayward winds no answer breathe,
No legend cometh from beneath
Of chief, with good sword at his side
Or Druid in his tomb of pride.

One quiet bird, that comes to make
Her lone nest in the scanty brake;
A nameless flower, a silent fern—
Lo! the dim stranger's storied urn.

Hark! on the cold wings of the blast
The future answereth to the past;
The bird, the flower, may gather still,
Thy voice shall cease upon the hill!

1834.

NOTE.

The word *tre* signifies in the ancient Cornish tongue "the place of abode," and *barrow* means "a burial mound." The word "Trebarrow" implies, therefore, "a dwelling among the graves;" and my house at North Tamerton was so named by me because it was surrounded by these green heaps of the dead. Some of these I opened, and in the centre of one of them I found an urn of baked clay filled with human ashes, and a patera, which I still possess, of the same material. It denotes in all likelihood the entombment of a Keltic priest, and that of pre-Christian times.

"PATER VESTER PASCIT ILLA."

OUR bark is on the waters! wide around,
   The wandering wave; above, the lonely sky.
Hush! a young sea-bird floats, and that quick cry
Shrieks to the levelled weapon's echoing sound,
Grasps its lank wing, and on, with reckless bound!
   Yet, creature of the surf, a sheltering breast
   To-night shall haunt in vain thy far-off nest,
A call unanswered, search the rocky ground.
   Lord of Leviathan! when Ocean heard,
Thy gathering voice, and sought his native breeze;
When whales first plunged with life, and the proud deep
Felt unborn tempests heave in troubled sleep;
   Thou didst provide, e'en for this nameless bird,
Home, and a natural love, amid the surging seas

August 25, 1835.

DEATH SONG.

THERE lies a cold corpse upon the sands
   Down by the rolling sea;
Close up the eyes and straighten the hands,
   As a Christian man's should be.

Bury it deep, for the good of my soul,
   Six feet below the ground;
Let the sexton come and the death-bell toll,
   And good men stand around.

Lay it among the churchyard stones,
    Where the priest hath blessed the clay;
I cannot leave the unburied bones,
    And I fain would go my way.

1835

THE SEA-BIRD'S CRY.

TIS harsh to hear, from ledge or peak,
    The cruel cormorant's tuneless shriek;
Fierce songs they chant, in pool or cave,
Dark wanderers of the western wave.
Here will the listening landsman pray
For memory's music, far away;
Soft throats that nestling with the rose,
Soothe the glad rivulet as it flows.

Cease, stranger! cease that fruitless word,
Give eve's hush'd bough to woodland bird:
Let the winged minstrel's valley-note,
'Mid flowers and fragrance, pause and float.
Here must the echoing beak prevail,
To pierce the storm, and cleave the gale;
To call, when warring tides shall foam,
The fledgeling of the waters home.

Wild things are here of sea and land,
Stern surges and a haughty strand;
Sea-monsters haunt yon cavern'd lair,
The mermaid wrings her briny hair.

That cry, those sullen accents sound
Like native echoes of the ground.
Lo! He did all things well Who gave
The sea-bird's voice to such a wave.

August 27, 1835.

[First printed in *Records of the Western Shore*, Second Series, 1836, then, with a few alterations, in *The Cornish Ballads*, 1869.—ED.]

MINSTER CHURCH
AND THE CONFIRMATION DAY,

AUGUST XVII., MDCCCXXXVI.

HANG not the harp upon the willow-bough,
    But teach thy native echoes one more song
Though fame withhold her sigil from thy brow,
And years half yield thee to the unnoted throng.
Doth not the linnet her meek lay prolong
In the lone depths of some deserted wood?
Springs not the violet coarse weeds among,
Where no fond voice shall praise her solitude?
Happy that bird and flower, though there be few intrude?

The Minster of the Trees! a lonely dell
Deep with old oaks, and 'mid their quiet shade,
Grey with the moss of years, yon antique cell!
Sad are those walls: The cloister lowly laid
Where pacing monks at solemn evening made
Their chanted orisons; and as the breeze
Came up the vale, by rock and tree delay'd,

They heard the awful voice of many seas
Blend with thy pausing hymn—thou Minster of the
    Trees![1]

The thoughts of days long past lie buried here;
Scenes of the former men my soul surround:
Lo! a dark priest, who bends with solemn ear—
A warrior prostrate on the awful ground,
Hark! by stern promise is Lord Bottreaux bound
To spread for Palestine his contrite sail;
In distant dreams to hear the vesper sound
Of that sweet bell; but never more to hail
Amidst those native trees, the Minster of the Vale![2]

Gaze yet again! A maid with hooded brow
Glides like a shadow through the cloister'd wood;
'Tis not to breathe Saint Ursula's stony vow
She haunts at eve that dreamy solitude;—
Yon gnarlèd oak was young, when there they stood,
The lady and the priest—they met to sigh:
For who be they with sudden grasp intrude?
They sever them in haste—yet not to die.
Hark! from yon stifled wall a low and frequent cry![3]

---

[1] An alien priory to the abbey of St. Sergius, at Angiers, once occupied this glen. When it was dissolved the chapel was suffered to remain. It still preserves a record of the monasteries in its name—"the minster church."

[2] On an artificial mound in the gorge of a valley, near this church, stood the castle of the Barons of Bottreaux; the name of their place of abode accrued to the surrounding village, which is now abbreviated into Boscastle [Bottreaux' Castle.]

[3] The doom of the immured is fearfully described in the second canto of "Marmion."

Long generations! lo, a ghastly man
Is leaning there, bent with the weight of days!
His cell was shattered by the reckless ban
Of a hard monarch—hush'd the voice of praise.
He had gone forth—strange faces met his gaze:
Ailric was dead, and cold was Edith's eye;
He had return'd—no sheltering roof to raise,
But 'mid the ruins of his love to die—
To pass from that worn frame into his native sky.

Wake! Dreamer of the Past;—no fairer grace
Dwelt in the vale or glided o'er the plain.
Heaven's changeless smile is here—earth's constant face;
The mingling sighs of woodland and the main.
Here, at lone eve, still seek this simple fane
Hearts that would cherish, 'midst their native trees,
A deathless faith—a hope that is not vain;
The tones that gather'd on the ancient breeze;
The Minster's pausing psalm; the chorus of the seas.

And lo! 'tis Holy Day!—through vale and wood
Beat joyful hearts; and white-rob'd forms are seen
Peopling with life the leafy solitude;
For He, of aspect mild yet stately mien,
The master-soul of a far loftier scene,
Hath come, beside that low-roof'd wall to stand,
Where the meek minster loves her bowers of green,
To breathe the Blessing on that rural band;
Proudly they hear those tones and see that lifted hand!

And we, who gaze and ponder, have we not
Thoughts new and strange, for fancy's future hour?
Shall no glad visions haunt this storied spot,
Glide from those boughs, and rest by yonder tower?
Yes; there shall be a spell of mightiest power
Breath'd o'er that ground—him will these groves recall
Who saw, unbent, the deadly battle lower,
Fair Sion's turrets shake, her bulwarks fall;
And foremost mann'd the breach and latest left the wall.

Fane of the woods, farewell! an holier thought
Henceforth be thine; with added beauty blest!
The presence of this day hath surely wrought
A charm immortal for thy home of rest.
Long may the swallow find her wonted nest
On thy grey walls; long may the breezes bear
The sounds of worship from thy happy breast;
The mind that shook whole senates hath been there;[4]
Strong be the soul of faith, and firm the voice of prayer.

August, 1836.

[4] A confirmation was held in this church by the Lord Bishop of the diocese [Bishop Phillpotts.—ED.], on Wednesday, the 17th day of August, 1836—a day which will long be an era to be remembered by the inhabitants of a secluded district, never before honoured by an episcopal visit.

[First printed for private circulation as a quarto pamphlet (six leaves), 1836). Then in *Records of the Western Shore*, Second Series, 1836, and in *Ecclesia*, 1840.]

MODRYB MARYA—AUNT MARY.

A CHRISTMAS CHANT.

In old and simple-hearted Cornwall, the household names "Uncle" and "Aunt" were uttered and used as they are to this day in many countries of the East, not only as phrases of kindred, but as words of kindly greeting and tender respect. It was in the spirit, therefore, of this touching and graphic usage, that they were wont on the Tamar side to call the Mother of God in their loyal language *Modryb Marya*, or Aunt Mary.

NOW of all the trees by the king's highway,
    Which do you love the best?
O! the one that is green upon Christmas Day,
    The bush with the bleeding breast.
Now the holly with her drops of blood for me:
For that is our dear Aunt Mary's tree.

Its leaves are sweet with our Saviour's Name,
    'Tis a plant that loves the poor:
Summer and winter it shines the same,
    Beside the cottage door.
O! the holly with her drops of blood for me:
For that is our kind Aunt Mary's tree.

'Tis a bush that the birds will never leave:
    They sing in it all day long;
But sweetest of all upon Christmas Eve,
    Is to hear the robin's song.
'Tis the merriest sound upon earth and sea:
For it comes from our own Aunt Mary's tree.

So, of all that grow by the king's highway,
  I love that tree the best;
'Tis a bower for the birds upon Christmas Day,
  The bush of the bleeding breast.
O! the holly with her drops of blood for me:
For that is our sweet Aunt Mary's tree.
1838.

MORWENNA STATIO.

The Stow, or the place, of St. Morwenna; hence the *Breviate, hodie,* Morwenstow.

MY Saxon shrine! the only ground
    Wherein this weary heart hath rest:
What years the birds of God have found
    Along thy walls their sacred nest!
The storm—the blast—the tempest shock,
    Have beat upon those walls in vain;
She stands—a daughter of the rock—
    The changeless God's eternal fane.

Firm was their faith, the ancient bands,
    The wise of heart in wood and stone;
Who reared, with stern and trusting hands,
    These dark grey towers of days unknown:
They fill'd these aisles with many a thought,
    They bade each nook some truth reveal:
The pillar'd arch its legends brought,
    A doctrine came with roof and wall.

Huge, mighty, massive, hard, and strong,
    Were the choice stones they lifted then:
The vision of their hope was long,
    They knew their God, those faithful men.
They pitch'd no tent for change or death,
    No home to last man's shadowy day;
There! there! the everlasting breath,
    Would breathe whole centuries away.

See now, along that pillar'd aisle,
    The graven arches, firm and fair:
They bend their shoulders to the toil,
    And lift the hollow roof in air.
A sign! beneath the ship we stand,
    The inverted vessel's arching side;
Forsaken—when the fisher-band
    Went forth to sweep a mightier tide.

Pace we the ground! our footsteps tread
    A cross—the builder's holiest form:
That awful couch, where once was shed
    The blood, with man's forgiveness warm.
And here, just where His mighty breast
    Throb'd the last agony away,
They bade the voice of worship rest,
    And white-robed Levites pause and pray.

Mark! the rich rose of Sharon's bowers
    Curves in the paten's mystic mould:
The lily, lady of the flowers,
    Her shape must yonder chalice hold.

MORWENNA STATIO.

Types of the Mother and the Son,
    The twain in this dim chancel stand;
The badge[1] of Norman banners, one
    And one a crest of English land.

How all things glow with life and thought,
    Where'er our faithful fathers trod!
The very ground with speech is fraught,
    The air is eloquent of God.
In vain would doubt or mockery hide
    The buried echoes of the past;
A voice of strength, a voice of pride,
    Here dwells amid the storm and blast.

Still points the tower, and pleads the bell;
    The solemn arches breathe in stone;
Window and wall have lips to tell
    The mighty faith of days unknown.
Yea! flood, and breeze, and battle-shock
    Shall beat upon this church in vain:
She stands, a daughter of the rock,
    The changeless God's eternal fane.

---

[1] The rose and the fleur-de-lys, adopted from Song of Solomon ii. 1, were used as ecclesiastical emblems some centuries before they were assumed into the shields of Normandy and England.

[From *Ecclesia*, 1840.]

THE SAINTLY NAMES.

SISTERS were they, the fair and holy twain,
    Marveena and Morwenna; and the vales
  And mountains of their birth were in wild Wales;
Thence came they in their youth across the main.
    King Breachan was their sire, and his sweet wife,
    Gladwise,[1] their mother, gave them love and life.
Virgins they lived and died—Oh not in vain!
    One meekly built a solitary cell,
    Where still her lingering memory loves to dwell,
In the old arches of grey Marham's fane.
    The other sought the sea: her pleasant place
    The pilgrim of the waters still may trace,
Where rock and headland watch the ocean-plain.
    Mark how their blended names in music flow,
    The Church of Marham, and Morwenna's Stow!
Let not the Dreamer-of-the-Past complain—
The Saints, the Sanctuaries, the Creed, this very day
    remain!

[1] Or Gladys.—ED.

[From *Reeds Shaken with the Wind*, 1843, where the title is "Marham Church and Morwenstow." Reprinted in *The Cornish Ballads*.]

THE LEGEND OF S. MORWENNA,

A.D. 850.

[Our readers may be pleased to compare Mr. Hawker's prose version of the preceding Legend; it is given as an Appendix to "The Quest of the Sangraal," 1864.—ED.]

THERE dwelt in Wales in the Ninth Age a Keltic King: Breachan by name—it was from him that the words *Brecon* and *Brechnock* received origin—and Gladwise was his wife and queen. They had—it is the record of Leland the Scribe—children twenty and four. Now these were either their own children, or they were, according to the usage of those days, the offspring of the Nobles of the land placed for loyal and learned nurture in the palace of the king, and so called the children of his house: of these Morwenna was one. Her name is also written Modwenna, and sounded Mōrrŏnă. She grew up wise, learned and holy above her generation; and it was evermore the strong desire of her soul to bring the barbarous and pagan people among whom she dwelt to the Christian Font. Now so it was that when Morwenna had grown up to saintly womanhood, there was a King of Saxon England and Ethelwolf was his noble name. He likewise had many children, and while he entrusted to the famous S. Swithin the guidance of his sons, he besought King Breachan to send Morwenna to become the teacher of the Princess Edith, and the other daughters of his house. She came: she sojourned in his palace long years; and she so gladdened the King by her goodness and her grace that at last he was fain to give her whatsoever she sought in his royal domains. Now the piece of ground, or The Acre of God, which was wont in those days to be set apart and hallowed for the site of a future Church, was called The Station, or in native speech The Stowe, of the Martyr or Saint who gave name or origin to the altar-stone. So on a certain day, thus said Morwenna to the King, "Largess! my Lord the King: Largess for God!" "Largess! my daughter," answered Ethelwolf like a prince, "be it whatsoever it may." Then said Morwenna, "Sir! there is a stern and stately headland in far Cornwall, rugged and tall; and it looks along the Severn Sea: they call it on that Shore, Hethnacliff; that is to say, The Raven's Crag, because it hath been long ages the haunt and the home of the Birds of Elias. Very often, in wild Wales, have I watched across the waters until the sun fell red upon that Cornish rock, and I have said in my vows, 'Alas! and would to God that a font might be hewn and an altar built among the stones by yonder barbarous hill.' Give me then, I beseech thee, my Lord the King! a Stowe for a Priest in that scenery of my prayer that so the saying of the Seer may come to pass—'In the place of dragons where each lay there shall be grass with reeds and rushes.'" Her voice was heard: her entreaty was fulfilled; they set up yonder font with the carven cable coiled around it in stone, in memory of the vessel of old anchored in the Galilean Sea. They built an altar there of gray and native rock, and they linked it with Morwenna's name, the Tender and the True: and so it is, that, notwithstanding the lapse of ten whole centuries of English time, at this very day, the bourne of many a pilgrim to the West is still The Station of Morwenna; or, in simple and Saxon phrase,

MORWENSTOW.

[It appears to have been issued as a quarto leaflet, with two engravings, printed at Penzance, 1850. See *Bibliotheca Cornubiensis*.]

THE VINE.

HEARKEN! There is in old Morwenna's shrine,
   (A lonely sanctuary of the Saxon days,
  Rear'd by the Severn sea for prayer and praise,)
Amid the carved work of the roof, a vine;
  Its root is where the eastern sunbeams fall,
  First in the chancel, then along the wall
Slowly it travels on, a leafy line,
  With here and there a cluster, and anon
  More and more grapes, until the growth hath gone
Through arch and aisle. Hearken! and heed the sign.
  See! at the altar-side the steadfast root,
  Mark well the branches, count the summer fruit:
So let a meek and faithful heart be thine,
And gather from that tree a parable divine.

1840.

[Printed in *Reeds Shaken by the Wind*, 1843, where it is headed "Ecclesiography," and reprinted in *Echoes from Old Cornwall*, 1846, as "The Stem and the Boughs."—ED.

THE WELL OF ST MORWENNA.

HERE dwelt in time long past, so legends tell,
    Holy Morwenna, guardian of this well.
Here, on the foreheads of our fathers, poured,
From this lone spring, the laver of the Lord.

If, traveller, thy happy spirit know
That awful Fount whence living waters flow,
Then hither come to draw: thy feet have found
Amidst these rocks a place of holy ground.

Here, while the surges stormed and raved the blast,
The grain of mustard-seed was meekly cast,
Till grew and multiplied that goodly tree—
Shrines in the vale and towers along the sea.

Then sigh one blessing, breathe a voice of praise
O'er the fond labour of departed days;
Tell the glad waters of the former fame,
And teach the joyful winds Morwenna's name.

[Printed in *Records of the Western Shore*, Second Series, 1836, as "An Inscription for St. Morwenna's Well, four years prior to the date (1840) assigned to this piece by Mr. Godwin."—ED.]

"I AM THE RESURRECTION AND THE LIFE? SAITH THE LORD!"

MAY, 1840.

WE stood beside an opening grave,
    By fair Morwenna's walls of grey:
Our hearts were hush'd—the God who gave
Had called a sister-soul away.
    Hark! what wild tones around us float:
    The chaunting cuckoo's double note!

We uttered there the solemn sound—
" Man that is born from flesh of Eve,
The banished flower of Eden's ground,
Hath but a little time to live;"—
    And still, amid each pausing word,
    The strange cry of that secret bird.

" Ashes to ashes—dust to dust "—
The last farewell we sadly said.
Our mighty hope—our certain trust—
The resurrection of the dead.
    Again, all air, it glides around,
    A voice!—the spirit of a sound.

A doctrine dwells in that deep tone;
A truth is borne on yonder wing;
Long years! long years! the note is known—
The blessèd messenger of spring!
    Thus saith that pilgrim of the skies:
    " Lo! all which dieth shall arise!"

Rejoice! though dull with wintry gloom
Love's sepulchre and sorrow's night,
The sun shall visit depth and tomb
A season of eternal light!
  Like the glad bosom of the rose,
  The mound shall burst—the grave unclose!

Yea! soothed by that unvarying song
What generations here have trod!
What winds have breathed that sound along,
Fit signal of the changeless God!
  Hark! yet again the echoes float,
  The chaunting cuckoo's double note!

[From *Ecclesia*, 1840.]

THE WESTERN SHORE.

"Nunc scio quid sit amor, duris in cotibus illum."

MDCCCXL.

THOU lovely land! where, kindling, throng
 Scenes that should breathe the soul of song;
Home of high hopes that once were mine
Of loftier verse and nobler line!

'Tis past—the quench'd volcano's tide
Sleeps well within the mountain-side;
Henceforth shall time's cold touch control
The warring Hecla of my soul.

Welcome! wild rock and lonely shore,
Where round my days dark seas shall roar;
And thy gray fane, Morwenna, stand
The beacon of the Eternal Land!

My glebe occupies a position of wild and singular beauty: its western boundary is the sea, skirted by tall and tremendous cliffs, and near their brink, with the exquisite taste of Ecclesiastical antiquity, is placed the church. The original and proper designation of the parish is Morwenstow—that is, Morwenna's Stow or Station—but it has been corrupted by recent usage, like many other local names. Halfway down a precipitous cliff near the church there still survives, with its perpetual water but ruined walls, the Well of Morwenna, an old baptismal fount; and another, the vicarage Well of St. John, is used in the church in regeneration to this day.

[Entitled "Cornwall" in Poems containing the Second Series of *Records of the Western Shore*, &c., 1836. The present version is from *Ecclesia*, 1840, where it stands as the opening poem.—ED.]

THE EXILE'S TEXT

JEREMIAH XXII. 16.

WEEP ye not for the dead: they sleep
    In hallowed slumbers, calm and deep;
Their bed, the scenery of their birth,
The dust around them, Hebrew earth!

They cease—and yet bemoan them not:
Their tombs are in the blessèd spot
Where hearth, and home, and altar stand,
With Aaron's shrine and Judah's land!

But weep ye sore for us: we go
Where rivers of the stranger flow,
And Gentile winds must bear along
The Lord's—the God of Jacob's song!

THE EXILE'S TEXT.

We travel to the graves unknown—
To die, in cities not our own;
False feet our sepulchres will tread,
A breathing nation of the dead.

Bel's loathsome land! and Nebo's sky!
Our flesh will shudder where we lie;—
Bone to his bone will cleave and creep
From the vile earth around our sleep.

But they—the dead by Jordan's stream—
They hear those waters where they dream:
The floods that fall by Abraham's cave,
And Rachel's tomb, and Isaac's grave!

Then mourn ye not for them: their sleep
Is pure and blessed, calm and deep;
But grieve, yea, grieve for us: we go
Where rivers of the stranger flow!

No more! no more! oh, never more
The hills, the trees, the ocean-shore!
Ah! Salem, Gilead, Lebanon,
The Lord, the Lord your God, is gone!

[From *Ecclesia*, 1840.]

HOME ONCE MORE!

"*They shall flee every one to his own land.*"—Jeremiah l. 16.

HOME! home once more! and every tree
    Looks with familiar face on me:
A smile comes o'er the accustomed hill,
A voice of welcome from the rill.

Home! home once more! but where are now
The bounding breast and brightening brow,
The footstep firm, the bearing bold,
Wherewith I trod these scenes of old?

These all are fled—and in their room
Thought thickens all things into gloom;
Along this path the listener hears
Feet heavy with the toil of years.

Yet cleaves my soul to this dear glen,
The old remembrance lives again,
The scene sighs with its former breath,
Like that old Ridley loved in death.[1]

---

[1] Who can read without emotion the last words of Ridley, written in his prison-house in Oxford, in memory of the "scenes that he had loved the best" during the life that he was about to forego for Jesus Christ his sake? Who that loves old Oxford can fail to be touched by the passage to which these lines refer:—"Farewell sweet Magdalen-walks in Oxford, where I did learn Saint Paul's Epistles by heart."

HOME ONCE MORE.

Here did I chaunt to many a wind,
The themes of God's eternal mind;
While the deep stream and thrilling birds
Made music 'mid those mighty words.

Here, oracles an echo found
Breathed, far away on Syrian ground,
By prophet-bards to whom were given
The lore and poetry of Heaven.

Here, too, would dreamy thoughts recall
Gesture and tone of saintly Paul,
Till fancy heard the iron bands
That shook upon his lifted hands.

All, all is gone—no longer roll
Vision and dream around my soul:
But, in their stead, float down the wind
These fragments of a broken mind.

Still, home once more; for in this dale
The dust of love will fondly dwell;
And scenes so dear in life shall hide
The hearts that death could not divide.

1840.

[Printed in *Ecclesia*, but not included in Mr. Godwin's collection.]

THE POOR MAN AND HIS PARISH CHURCH.

A TRUE TALE.

THE poor have hands, and feet, and eyes,
    Flesh, and a feeling mind :
They breathe the breath of mortal sighs,
    They are of human kind.
They weep such tears as others shed,
    And now and then they smile :—
For sweet to them is that poor bread,
    They win with honest toil.

The poor men have their wedding-day :
    And children climb their knee :
They have not many friends, for they
    Are in such misery.
They sell their youth, their skill, their pains,
    For hire in hill and glen :
The very blood within their veins,
    It flows for other men.

They should have roofs to call their own,
    When they grow old and bent :
Meek houses built of dark grey stone,
    Worn labour's monument.
There should they dwell, beneath the thatch,
    With threshold calm and free :
No stranger's hand should lift the latch,
    To mark their poverty.

Fast by the church those walls should stand,
   Her aisles in youth they trod :—
They have no home in all the land,
   Like that old House of God.
There, there, the Sacrament was shed,
   That gave them heavenly birth ;
And lifted up the poor man's head
   With princes of the earth.

There in the chancel's voice of praise,
   Their simple vows were poured ;
And angels looked with equal gaze
   On Lazarus and his Lord.
There, too, at last, they calmly sleep,
   Where hallow'd blossoms bloom ;
And eyes as fond and faithful weep
   As o'er the rich man's tomb.

They told me of an ancient home,
   Beside a churchyard wall,
Where roses round the porch would roam,
   And gentle jasmines fall :
There dwelt an old man, worn and blind,
   Poor, and of lowliest birth ;
He seemed the last of all his kind—
   He had no friend on earth.

Men saw him till his eyes grew dim,
   At morn and evening tide
Pass, 'mid the graves, with tottering limb,
   To the grey chancel's side :

There knelt he down, and meekly prayed
    The prayers his youth had known:
Words by the old Apostles made,
    In tongues of ancient tone.

At matin-time, at evening hour,
    He bent with reverent knee:
The dial carved upon the tower
    Was not more true than he.
This lasted till the blindness fell
    In shadows round his bed;
And on those walls he loved so well,
    He looked, and they were fled.

Then would he watch, and fondly turn,
    If feet of men were there,
To tell them how his soul would yearn
    For the old place of prayer;
And some would lead him on to stand,
    While fast their tears would fall,
Until he felt beneath his hand
    The long-accustomed wall.

Then joy in those dim eyes would melt;
    Faith found the former tone;
His heart within his bosom felt
    The touch of every stone.
He died—he slept beneath the dew,
    In his own grassy mound:
The corpse, within the coffin, knew
    That calm, that holy ground.

THE POOR MAN AND HIS PARISH CHURCH

I know not why—but when they tell
   Of houses fair and wide,
Where troops of poor men go to dwell
   In chambers side by side :—
I dream of that old cottage door,
   With garlands overgrown,
And wish the children of the poor
   Had flowers to call their own.

And when they vaunt, that in those walls
   They have their worship-day,
Where the stern signal coldly calls
   The prisoned poor to pray,—
I think upon that ancient home
   Beside the churchyard wall,
Where roses round the porch would roam,
   And gentle jasmines fall.

I see the old man of my lay,
   His grey head bowed and bare;
He kneels by one dear wall to pray,
   The sunlight in his hair.
Well! they may strive, as wise men will,
   To work with wit and gold:
I think my own dear Cornwall still
   Was happier of old.

O! for the poor man's church again,
   With one roof over all;
Where the true hearts of Cornish men
   Might beat beside the wall:

The altars where, in holier days,
    Our fathers were forgiven,
Who went, with meek and faithful ways,
    Through the old aisles to heaven.

1840.

[Printed privately in leaflet form in 1843, and published in *Reeds Shaken with the Wind. The Second Cluster.* 1844. Reprinted in *Eckoes from Old Cornwall*, and in *The Cornish Ballads*.—ED.]

THE SONG OF THE SCHOOL:
ST. MARK'S, MORWENSTOW.

SING to the Lord the children's hymn,
    His gentle love declare,
Who bends amid the seraphim,
    To hear the children's prayer.

He at a mother's breast was fed,
    Though God's own Son was He;
He learnt the first small words He said
    At a meek mother's knee.

He held us to His mighty breast,
    The children of the earth;
He lifted up His hands and blessed
    The babes of human birth.

So shall He be to us our God,
    Our gracious Saviour too;
The scenes we tread His footsteps trod,
    The paths of youth He knew.

Lo! from the stars His face will turn
    On us with glances mild:
The angels of His presence yearn
    To bless the little child.

Keep us, O Jesu Lord, for Thee,
    That so, by Thy dear grace,
We, children of the font, may see
    Our heavenly Father's face.

Sing to the Lord the children's hymn,
    His tender love declare,
Who bends amid the seraphim,
    To hear the children's prayer.

1840.

[From *Reeds Shaken by the Wind*. 1843, and reprinted in *Echoes from Old Cornwall*, and *The Cornish Ballads*. Probably issued originally as a leaflet for school use.—ED.]

ON THE GRAVE OF A CHILD IN MORWENSTOW CHURCHYARD.

THOSE whom God loves die young;
    They see no evil days;
No falsehood taints their tongue,
    No wickedness their ways.

Baptized, and so made sure
    To win their safe abode;
What could we pray for more?
    They die, and are with God.

1840.

[In *Echoes from Old Cornwall*, 1846, and *The Cornish Ballads*, 1869.]

THE TAMAR SPRING.

The source of this storied river of the West is on a rushy knoll, in a moorland of this parish. The Torridge also flows from the self-same mound.

FOUNT of a rushing river! wild flowers wreathe
    The home where thy first waters sunlight claim;
The lark sits hushed beside thee, while I breathe,
    Sweet Tamar spring! the music of thy name.

On! through the goodly channel, on! to the sea!
    Pass amid heathery vale, tall rock, fair bough:
But never more with footsteps pure and free,
    Or face so meek with happiness as now.

Fair is the future scenery of thy days,
    Thy course domestic, and thy paths of pride:
Depths that give back the soft-eyed violet's gaze,
    Shores where tall navies march to meet the tide.

Thine, leafy Tetcott, and those neighbouring walls,
    Noble Northumberland's embowered domain;
Thine, Cartha Martha, Morwell's rocky falls,
    Storied Cotehele, and Ocean's loveliest plain.

Yet false the vision, and untrue the dream,
    That lures thee from thy native wilds to stray:
A thousand griefs will mingle with that stream,
    Unnumbered hearts shall sigh those waves away.

Scenes fierce with men, thy seaward current laves,
   Harsh multitudes will throng thy gentle brink;
Back! with the grieving concourse of thy waves,
   Home! to the waters of thy childhood shrink!

Thou heedest not! thy dream is of the shore,
   Thy heart is quick with life; On! to the sea!
How will the voice of thy far streams implore
   Again amid these peaceful weeds to be!

My Soul! my Soul! a happier choice be thine—
   Thine the hushed valley, and the lonely sod;
False dreams, far vision, hollow hope resign,
   Fast by our Tamar spring, alone with God!

[This poem is entitled "That Ancient River," with reference to Judges v. 21, in *Ecclesia*, 1840, and Mr. Godwin, therefore, assigned that date to its production: it is quoted in *Footprints of Former Men*, 1870, and in *The Cornish Ballads*, 1869. It was, however, first printed in the second series of *Records of the Western Shore*, 1836, as "The Source of the Tamar," with some verbal differences.—ED.]

THE STORM.

WAR, 'mid the ocean and the land!
    The battle-field, Morwenna's strand,
Where rock and ridge the bulwark keep,
The giant-warders of the deep.

They come! and shall they not prevail,
The seething surge, the gathering gale?
They fling their wild flag to the breeze,
The banner of a thousand seas.

THE STORM.

They come—they mount—they charge in vain,
Thus far, incalculable main!
No more! thine hosts have not o'erthrown
The lichen on the barrier stone.

Have the rocks faith, that thus they stand,
Unmoved, a grim and stately band,
And look, like warriors tried and brave,
Stern, silent, reckless, o'er the wave?

Have the proud billows thoughts and life,
To feel the glory of the strife;
And trust, one day, in battle bold,
To win the foeman's haughty hold?

Mark where they writhe with pride and shame,
Fierce valour, and the zeal of fame!
Hear how their din of madness raves,
The baffled army of the waves!

Thy way, O God, is in the sea,
Thy paths, where awful waters be;
Thy spirit thrills the conscious stone:
O Lord, thy footsteps are not known!

1840.

[Printed in *Ecclesia*, 1840, in *Echoes from Old Cornwall*, and *The Cornish Ballads*, and in the "Remembrances of a Cornish Vicar," (*Footsteps of Former Men in Far Cornwall*, 1870).—ED.]

THE CELL BY THE SEA

HOW wildly sweet by Hartland Tower,
   The thrilling voice of prayer:
A seraph, from his cloudy bower,
   Might lean to listen there.

For time, and place, and storied days,
   To that great fane have given
Hues that might win an angel's gaze,
   'Mid scenery of heaven.

Above—the ocean breezes sweep,
   With footsteps firm and free:
Around—the mountains guard the deep,
   Beneath—the wide, wide sea.

Enter! the arching roofs expand,
   Like vessels on the shore;
Inverted, when the fisher-band
   Might tread their planks no more

But reared on high in that stern form,
   Lest faithless hearts forget
The men that braved the ancient storm,
   And hauled the early net.

The tracery of a quaint old time
   Still weaves the chancel screen:
And tombs, with many a broken rhyme,
   Suit well this simple scene.

A Saxon font, with baptism bright,
    The womb of mystic birth,
An altar, where, in angels' sight,
    Their Lord descends to earth.

Here glides the spirit of the psalm,
    Here breathes the soul of prayer:
The awful church—so hushed—so calm—
    Ah! surely God is there.

And lives no legend on the wall?
    No theme of former men?
A shape to rise at fancy's call,
    And sink in graves again?

Yes! there, through yonder portal stone,
    With whisper'd words they tell,
How once the monk, with name unknown,
    Prepared that silent cell.

He came with griefs that shunned the light,
    With vows long breathed in vain:
Those arches heard, at dead of night,
    The lash, the shriek, the pain;

The prayer that rose and fell in tears,
    The sob, the bursting sigh:
Till woke, with agony of years,
    The exceeding bitter cry.

This lasted long—as life will wear,
    E'en though in anguish nurs'd—
Few think what human hearts can bear
    Before their sinews burst.

It lasted long—but not for aye :
　　The hour of freedom came :
In that dim niche the stranger lay
　　A cold and silent frame.

What sorrows shook the strong man's soul,
　　What guilt was rankling there,
We know not : time may not unroll
　　The page of his despair.

He sleeps in yonder nameless ground,
　　A cross hath marked the stone ;
Pray ye, his soul in death hath found
　　The peace to life unknown.

And if ye mourn that man of tears,
　　Take heed, lest ye too fall ;
A day may mar the rest, that years
　　Shall seek but not recall.

Nor think that deserts soothe despair,
　　Or shame in cells is screen'd ;
For Thought, the demon, will be there,
　　And Memory, the fiend.

Then waft, ye winds, this tale of fear,
　　Breathe it in hall and bower,
Till reckless hearts grow hushed to hear,
　　The Monk of Hartland Tower.

[Printed in *Ecclesia,* 1840, in *Echoes from Old Cornwall, The Cornish Ballads, &c.*]

EPHPHATHA.

HIGH matins now in bower and hall!
    It is the Baptist's festival:
What showers of gold the sunbeams rain,
Through the tall window's purple pane!
What rich hues on the pavement lie,
A molten rainbow from the sky!

But light and shadow loveliest fall
Yonder, along the southward wall,
Where ceased, e'en now, the chaunted hymn
Of that grey man whose eyes are dim:
'Twas an old legend, quaintly sung,
Caught from some far barbaric tongue.

He asks, and bread of wheat they bring;
He thirsts for water from the spring
Which flowed of old and still flows on,
With name and memory of St. John:
So fares the pilgrim in that hall,
E'en on the Baptist's festival.

" How sad a sight is blind old age!"
Thus said the lady's youthful page:
" He eats, but sees not on that bread
What glorious radiance there is shed;
He drinks from out that chalice fair,
Nor marks the sunlight glancing there."

" Watch! gentle Ronald, watch and pray!
And hear once more an old man's lay:

I cannot see the morning pour'd,
Ruddy and rich on this gay board;
I may not trace the noonday light,
Wherewith my bread and bowl are bright:

"But thou, whose words are sooth, hast said,
That brightness falls on this fair bread;
Thou sayest—and thy tones be true—
This cup is tinged with heaven's own hue:
I trust thy voice; I know from thee
That which I cannot hear nor see.

"Watch! gentle Ronald, watch and pray!
It is the Baptist's holy day!
Go, where in old Morwenna's shrine,
They break the bread and bless the wine;
There meekly bend thy trusting knee,
And touch what sight can never see.

"Thou wilt behold, thy lips may share
All that the cup and paten bear;
But life unseen moves o'er that bread,
A glory on that wine is shed;
A light comes down to breathe and be,
Though hid, like summer suns, from me.

"Watch! gentle Ronald, watch and pray!
Day oft is night and night is day:
The arrowy glance of lady fair
Beholds not things that throng the air;
The clear bright eye of youthful page
Hath duller ken than blind old age."

'Tis evensong in bower and hall
On the bold Baptist's festival;
The harp is husht and mute the hymn,
The guest is gone whose eyes are dim,
But evermore to Ronald clung
That mystic measure, quaintly sung.

June 24th, 1840.

"I have sought in these verses, to suggest a shadow of that beautiful instruction to Christian men, the actual and spiritual presence of our Lord in the second Sacrament of his Church; a primal and perpetual doctrine in the faith once delivered to the Saints. How sadly the simplicity of this hath and has been distorted and disturbed by the gross and sensuous notion of a carnal presence introduced by the Romish innovation of the eleventh century!"—Note in *Ecclesia*. 1841.

"I have sought in these verses, to suggest the manner of that miraculous event, the actual and etherial Presence of Our LORD in the Second Sacrament of His Church."—Note in *Echoes from Old Cornwall*, 1846.

[These notes are omitted by Mr. Godwin.—ED.]

THE SIGNALS OF LEVI.

The Rabbins have ruled that the daily oblation was never to begin until the Signal of Levi was heard, and the time was thus to be known: A Levite was placed, before cockcrow, on the roof of the Temple, to watch the sky; and when the day had so far dawned that he could see Hebron, a city on the heights where John the Baptizer was afterwards born, then he blew with his trumpet an appointed sound, and the sacrifice began.

SIGNAL THE FIRST

THERE is light on Hebron now:
    Hark to the trumpet din!
Day dawns on Hebron's brow,
    Let the sacrifice begin.

THE SIGNALS OF LEVI.

Hear ye the gathering sound!
   How the lute and harp rejoice,
'Mid the roar of oxen bound,
   And the lamb's beseeching voice.

This day both prince and priest
   Will hold at Salem's shrine
A high and haughty feast
   Of flesh and the ruddy wine.

For a perilous hour is fled,
   And the fear is vain at last,
Though foretold by sages dead,
   And sworn by the Prophets past.

They said that a mortal birth
   E'en now would a Name unfold
That should rule the wide, wide earth,
   And quench the thrones of old.

But no sound, nor voice, nor word,
   The tale of travail brings;
Not an infant cry is heard
   In the palaces of kings.

Blossom and branch are bare
   On Jesse's stately stem:
So they bid swart Edom [1] wear
   Fallen Israel's diadem.

[1] The Herods were of Idumean race.

How they throng the cloistered ground
  'Mid Judah's shame and sin:
Hark to the trumpet-sound!
  Let the sacrifice begin.

Signal the Second

There is light on Hebron's towers,
  Day dawns o'er Jordan's stream,
And it floats where Bethlehem's bowers
  Of the blessèd morning dream.

Yet it wakes no kingly halls
  It cleaves no purple room;
The soft, calm radiance falls
  On a cavern's vaulted gloom.

But there, where the oxen rest
  When the weary day is done,
How that maiden-mother's breast
  Thrills with her Awful Son!

A cave where the fatlings roam,
  By the ruddy heifer trod,
Yea! the mountain's rifted home
  Is the birthplace of a God!

This is He! the mystic birth
  By the sign and voice foretold;
He shall rule the wide, wide earth,
  And quench the thrones of old.

The Child of Judah's line,
  The son of Abraham's fame:
Arise, ye lands! and shine
  With the blessèd Jesu's name.

This is the glorious dawn:
  So fades the night of sin;
Lo! the gloom of death is gone,
  Let the sacrifice begin.

Signal the Third

" Oh! watchman! what of the night?
  Tell, Christian soldier, tell:
Are Hebron's towers in sight?
  Hast thou watched and warded well?"

" Yea; we have paced the wall
  Till the day-star's glimmering birth;
And we breathed our trumpet-call
  When the sunlight waked the earth."

" What sawest thou with the dawn?
  Say, Christian warder, say:
When the mists of night were gone,
  And the hills grew soft with day?"

" We beheld the morning swell
  Bright o'er the eastern sea;
Till the rushing sunbeams fell
  Where the westward waters be.

"City and bulwark lay
   Rich with the orient blaze,
And rocks, at the touch of day,
   Gave out a sound of praise.

"No hill remained in cloud,
   There lurked no darkling glen;
And the voice of God was loud
   Upon every tongue of men.

"There shall never more be night
   With this eternal sun;
There be Hebrons many in sight,
   And the sacrifice is done!"

1840.

[From *Ecclesia*, 1840. Also reprinted in the other collections of Mr. Hawker's Poems, and in *Lyra Mystica* (Rev. Orby Shipley), 1865, pp. 148—52.—ED.]

THE CHILD JESUS.

A CORNISH CAROL.

WELCOME that Star in Judah's sky,
   That voice o'er Bethlehem's palmy glen:
The lamp, far sages hailed on high,
   The tones that thrill'd the shepherd men:
Glory to God in highest heaven!
   Thus Angels smote the echoing chord;
Glad tidings unto man forgiven!
   Peace from the presence of the Lord!

The Shepherds sought that Birth divine,
   The Wise Men traced their guided way;
There by strange light and mystic sign,
   The God they came to worship lay.
A human Babe in beauty smiled,
   Where lowing oxen round Him trod:
A maiden clasped her Awful Child,
   Pure offspring of the breath of God.

Those voices from on high are mute;
   The Star the Wise Men saw is dim;
But Hope still guides the wanderer's foot,
   And Faith renews the angel-hymn:
Glory to God in loftiest heaven!
   Touch with glad hand the ancient chord;
Good tidings unto man forgiven,
   Peace from the presence of the Lord!

[From *Ecclesia*, 1840. Also in *Lyra Messianica* (Rev. Orby Shipley), 1864, pp. 86–7. First printed in *Records of the Western Shore*, second series, 1836.—ED.]

THE WAIL OF THE CORNISH MOTHER.

"In Ramah there was a voice heard."

THEY say 'tis a sin to sorrow—
   That what God doth is best:
But 'tis only a month to-morrow,
   I buried it from my breast.

I know it should be a pleasure,
   Your child to God to send ;
But mine was a precious treasure
   To me and to my poor friend.¹

I thought it would call me " mother,"
   The very first words it said ;
Oh ! I never can love another
   Like the blessèd babe that's dead.

Well, God is its own dear Father,
   It was carried to church and blessed :
And our Saviour's arms will gather
   Such children to their rest.

I shall make my best endeavour
   That my sins may be forgiven ;
I will serve God more than ever,
   To meet my child in heaven.

I will check this foolish sorrow,
   For what God does is best ;
But Oh ! 'tis a month to-morrow,
   I buried it from my breast.

¹ The name for Husband in this country.

[Printed in *Ecclesia*, 1840, as " The Cornish Mother's Grief " ; the fourth verse was added in *The Cornish Ballads*, 1879, wherein the title stands as above. First printed in the second series of *Records of the Western Shore*, 1836, as " The Cornish Mother's Lament."—ED.]

TO HIS ROYAL HIGHNESS THE PRINCE ALBERT OF SAXE-COBURG AND GOTHA.

HE comes! a Conqueror! with the soft control
    Mightier than warrior's sword in monarch's hand;
He comes! to claim the Lady of his soul—
    A fearless knight from the old German land!

A voice of welcome from a thousand hills!
    The sound of love in earth and air and sea!
A nation's heart, thy name, Prince Albert! fills
    With prayer and blessing for thy Bride and thee!

Thou comest to link thee with a lofty soil,
    A land of graceful dames and stately men:
Be proud! on thee will England's Daughter smile,
    And thou on England's Queen look love again.

What haughty dreams thy gathering visions yield!
    'Tis thine the awful couch of kings to share;
The hope of many a land thine arm must shield,
    The Beauty of our Isles shall slumber there!

Bring princes in thy breast across the brine!
    Lo, round the chaste form of thy noble mate
The future spirits of a shadowy line,
    The souls of kings unborn, in silence wait!

TO PRINCE ALBERT.

Forget thy father-land! Thou hast no more
    Another city, hearth, or native home:
This is thy country, this thy natural shore,
    Thine eagle-nest amid the ocean-foam.

Come! at an English altar proudly stand—
    Take, from our ancient priest, thy chosen bride!
Breathe, in the language of thy Lady's land,
    The eternal vows—the pledge of love and pride!

Rejoice, O Prince! her Fathers' Faith is thine,
    One worship and one creed ye twain will share;
How many a solemn arch and cloistered shrine
    Shall hail your blended names in English prayer![1]

Love well our clime! the scenery of thy choice,
    Thy Lady's isle—the pride of earth and sea;
Her fanes will greet thee with their holiest voice,
    Her towers among the trees shall thrill for thee!

'Tis not the troth of state—the plighted hands
    Where passion shudders at the feet of pride;
No selfish bridegroom at yon altar stands,
    Nor glitters there a cold and reckless bride!

Joy to that fane! the noble and the fair
    Are met to blend the tones of love and truth.
Joy to that fane! an English lady there
    Binds to her soul the husband of her youth.

[1] This was written on the supposition that the Prince would be named in the liturgy.

He comes, as came the mighty hearts of old,
  The men of bounding steed and belted brand;
That which his vows have won his arm shall hold—
  A fearless knight from the old German land !

The voice of welcome, Prince ! I wake once more,—
  Far from the glare of courts, from cities free,
A lowly name, on Cornwall's rocky shore,
  I breathe this blessing for thy Bride and thee !

January, 8th, 1840.

Printed privately, first, as a pamphlet ; then in *Ecclesia*, 1840 ; but scored-out by Mr Hawker's hand in his own copy of the latter work, and marked "Trash ! R. S. H." It has not been reprinted in any of the author's own collections.—ED.]

THE SECOND BIRTH OF THE PRINCESS ROYAL OF ENGLAND—VICTORIA ADELAIDE MARY LOUISA.

"King's daughters were among thy honourable women."
Ps. xlv, 9.

GOLD ! ruddy, rich, and rare !
  With silver from the mine—
The gems of price are glorious there,
  And costly vessels shine ;
And storied walls are nobly spread
With fair forms of the living dead !

Bright brow and graceful mien !
  The guests of bower and hall—
They come to watch a sacred scene,
  The solemn festival—

A proud and stately host they stand,
The kingly blood of English land.

A priest ! a man grown old,
   With voice of ancient tone,
And agèd arms, that fain must hold
   The offspring of a throne ;
That voice shall greet, those hands will bless
The flower of England's loveliness.

A prayer—a vow—the sign—
   The mystic waters poured :
And lo! the child of earthly line
   Is daughter of the Lord !
What glories fill—what wonders haunt
The rich breast of that silvery font !—

Yet from no native streams,
   Though beautiful they be—
From no glad river, as it gleams,
   A pilgrim to the sea :
They will not lave from English springs
The daughter of a thousand kings.

River of lordly Dan ![1]
   Thine was the chosen bed ;
The glory of thy waters ran
   Around that infant head ;
'Twas thou ! with life, and breath, and fame,
Proud memories, and a mighty name.

Thou ! that in ancient days
   Didst hear the voice of God,

---

[1] The name Jordan signifies the river of Dan.

And fleddest ; while thy torrent-ways
  The hosts of Israel trod.[2]
Thy gentle waters, pure and mild,
Fell softly on that happy child !

Thou ! that of old didst lave
  The Maiden's Awful Birth [3]
Even He that made thy Syrian wave
  The glory of the earth !—
See ! o'er her brow thy fountains glide—
Her own dear Saviour's blessèd tide !

Keep, child of England's fame,
  The blessing and the vow:
The mighty thought, what waters came
  To touch thine infant brow :
Lo ! Jordan rolls beyond the sea,
Bright babe, with memory of thee !

Red gold that brow may bind,
  Gems 'mid thy beauty shine,
Around that form rich robes be twined
  With silver from the mine :
But fairer fall, and lovelier gleam
The starry dews of Syria's stream !

[2] Joshua iii. 13.

[3] "Then cometh Jesus from Galilee to Jordan unto John, to be baptized of him."—St. Matt. iii. 13.

Circa 1840.

[Printed in *Reeds Shaken by the Wind. The First Cluster*, 1843, wherein, in Mr. Hawker's own copy, the first verse is scored out, in red ink, with the emphatic word "Trash, R.S.H."—ED.]

DUTY DONE.

WILD is the vale of Tidna; bleak and bare
    The rugged rocks that stand in silence there;
And one small brook, with meek and quiet song,
Glides, like a dream, those nameless banks along;
Yet might those waters if their tale were told
A doctrine teach—a mystery unfold!
Far, far away that river's place of birth,
Mid weeds and waving flowers, its native earth;
Onward it came, and gathering as it passed,
Grew from a fountain to a stream at last;
Until, to strength increas'd—to manhood grown,
It turn'd the upper and the nether stone!
A duteous course the faithful water ran,
The vassal of the mighty master, Man.
Their aim achieved—their lowly duty done,
Thenceforward, on the rushing waters run,
And at the last with patient lapse they glide
To Ocean's shore and mingle with the tide.
    Be this, my soul, a parable to thee,
    Thus make thy courses, and so meet the sea!

[This was found in a MS. book dated 1836. It is probably the germ-thought of "The Token-stream of Tidnacombe," and is now printed for the first time.—ED.]

THE TOKEN STREAM OF TIDNA COMBE.

A SOURCE of gentle waters, mute and mild,
    A few calm reeds around the sedgy brink,
The loneliest bird, that flees to waste or wild,
    Might fold its feathers here in peace to drink.

I do remember me of such a scene,
    Far in the depths of memory's glimmering hour,
When earth looked e'en on me with tranquil mien,
    And life gushed, like this fountain in her bower.

But lo! a little on, a gliding stream,
    Fed with fresh rills from fields before unknown,
Where the glad roses on its banks may dream
    The watery mirror spreads for them alone.

Ah! Woe is me! that flood, those flowers, recall
    A gleaming glimpse of Time's departed shore,
Where now no dews descend, no sunbeams fall,
    And leaf and blossom burst, no more, no more!

See now! with heart more stern, and statelier force,
    Through Tidna's vale the river leaps along;
The strength of many trees shall guard its course,
    Birds in the branches soothe it with their song.

O type of a far scene! the lovely land
    Where youth wins many a friend, and I had one;
Still do thy bulwarks, dear old Oxford, stand?
    Yet, Isis, do thy thoughtful waters run?

But hush! a spell is o'er thy conscious wave,
   Pause and move onward with obedient tread ;
At yonder wheel they bind thee for their slave,
   Hireling of man, they use thy toil for bread.

Still is thy stream an image of the days
   At duty's loneliest labour meekly bound ;
The foot of joy is hush'd, the voice of praise,
   We twain have reached the stern and anxious ground.

And now what hills shall smile, what depths remain,
   Thou tamed and chastened wanderer, for thee?
A rocky path, a solitary plain
   Must be thy broken channel to the sea.

Come then, sad river, let our footsteps blend
   Onward, by silent bank, and nameless stone:
Our years began alike, so let them end,—
   We live with many men, we die alone.

Why dost thou slowly wind and sadly turn,
   As loth to leave e'en this most joyless shore?
Doth thy heart fail thee? do thy waters yearn
   For the far fields of memory once more?

Ah me! my soul, and thou art treacherous too,
   Linked to this fatal flesh, a fettered thrall:
The sin, the sorrow, why would'st thou renew?
   The past, the perish'd, vain and idle all!

Away! behold at last the torrent leap,
   Glad, glad to mingle with yon foamy brine;
Free and unmourn'd, the cataract cleaves the steep—
   O river of the rocks, thy fate is mine!

[From *Ecclesia*, 1840, reprinted in *The Cornish Ballads*.]

THE BUTTERFLY.

BIRD of the moths! that radiant wing
    Hath borne thee from thine earthly lair;
Thou revellest on the breath of spring,
    A graceful shape of woven air!

The glories of the earth are thine,
    The joyful breeze, the balmy sky;
For thee the starry roses shine,
    And violets in their valleys sigh.

Yet was the scene as soft and bright
    When thou wert low in wormy rest:
The skies of summer gushed with light,
    The blossoms breathed on Nature's breast.

But thou that gladness didst not share,
    A cave restrained that shadowy form;
In vain did fragrance fill the air,
    Dew soften and the sunbeams warm.

Dull was thy day—a living death,
    Till the great change in glory came,
And thou, a thing of life and breath,
    Didst cleave the air with quivering frame!

    *   *   *   *

My son! my son! read, mark, and learn
    This parable of summer skies,
Until thy trusting spirit yearn,
    Like the bright moth, to rush and rise.

Lo! round and near, a mightier scene,
  With hues that flesh may not behold!
There all things glow with loveliest mien,
  And earthly forms have heavenly mould!

Oh! for that place of paths divine,
  By the freed soul in rapture trod;
The upper air, the fields that shine,
  For ever in the Light of God!

"The earnest expectation of the creature waiteth for the manifestation of the sons of God."—Romans viii. 19.

[From *Ecclesia*, 1840.]

CONFIRMATION

"Lo! this hath touched."—Isaiah vi. 7.

He lifts the appointed hand! He breathes the tone
That none but Apostolic lips may own;
Yea! in yon fane by hallowing footsteps trod,
He claims and binds the eternal troth of God!

Keep, youthful pilgrim, keep that pledge and vow,
Heaven's chosen touch hath blest thy happy brow;
E'en as the coal from off the altar came,
To wake on prophet lips the kindling flame!

Let no heart falter, and no footstep stray;
Firm be the onward path and pure the way;
Long let the banners bear the conquering sign,
March, Christian soldier, march! the ranks of God
    are thine!

[From *Ecclesia*, 1840. Probably issued originally as a leaflet for candidates.—ED.]

"ARE THEY NOT ALL MINISTERING SPIRITS?"

WE see them not—we cannot hear
    The music of their wing—
Yet know we that they sojourn near,
    The Angels of the spring!

They glide along this lovely ground,
    When the first violet grows;
Their graceful hands have just unbound
    The zone of yonder rose!

I gather it for thy dear breast,
    From stain and shadow free,
That which an Angel's touch hath blest
    Is meet, my love, for thee!

[From *Ecclesia*, 1840.]

THE FONT.

RAISE ye the sacred hand! and proudly shower
  The rain of God upon the mortal flower!
Lo! One unseen shall in those waters blend,
And with a breathing dove's fond wing descend.

Suffer the little child! the wide, wide earth
Shall yield no happier hour for heavenly birth;
What fairer shrine can woo the God to rest
Than the meek altar of that infant breast?

[From *Ecclesia*, 1840.]

THE NUN OF CARMEL'S LAMENT
AT THE
CONQUEST OF ST. JEAN D'ACRE.
NOVEMBER 2, 1840.

WEEPEST thou! weepest thou! with victory
  won,
Dark-eyed daughter of the Syrian sun!
Where Carmel, a conqueror, cleaves the sky,
With the turban'd palm for his crest on high.

Tears! where the crescent moon is bright,
And the red, red cross hath prevail'd in fight,
And swarthy Misraim's doom is done,
And Syria is safe, and Acco[1] won!

[1] The ancient name (*cf.* Judges i. 31) of St. Jean d'Acre.

THE NUN OF CARMEL'S LAMENT.

I weep not the home of my Syrian birth,
Nor the victor's foot on my fathers' earth,
Nor the rushing rivers of Gentile gore,
That darken the floods upon Jewry's shore.

But I grieve that the sweet and the holy Sign
With the Moslem banner should wave and shine;
I blush for the battle that blends in fame
Mohammed's and Isa Ben Mariam's[2] name.

Woe worth the war where the gain is loss!
Shame to the Crescent beside the Cross!
Trouble and dread to the pledge that gave
A Christian arm to a Pagan glaive!

I dream of the hearts that are lowly laid,
The warriors that wielded the beamy blade,
And waved to the winds yon blessèd sign,
In war for their God and his tarnished shrine.

I think on the days that are quench'd and gone,
When the souls of England came sternly on,
To sweep from the lands the accursèd horde
That mock'd at the Cross and blasphemed its Lord.

And I see where the Turkish cohorts ride—
The armies of Christ—they are side by side!
And I hear, in the city's funeral knell,
Old England's shout and the Islam yell.

[2] The Syriac name of Jesus, Son of Mary.

Tears then, and grief, for the Syrian sun,
With victory gained and with Acco won.
Oh! pride will be shame and triumph loss
Till the Crescent shiver beneath the Cross!

November, 1840.

[From *Ecclesia*, 1840.]

THE RINGERS OF LANCELL'S TOWERS.

These ancient men rang at the accession of George the Third and all again at his jubilee. Three of them lived on to ring in George the Fourth; and two survived to celebrate, in their native tower, the coronation of King William the Fourth.

THEY meet once more! that ancient band,
With furrow'd cheek and failing hand;
One peal to-day they fain would ring,
The jubilee of England's king!

They meet once more! but where are now
The sinewy arm, the laughing brow,
The strength that hailed, in happier times,
King George the Third with lusty chimes?

Yet proudly gaze on that lone tower,
No goodlier sight hath hall or bower;
Meekly they strive—and closing day
Gilds with soft light their locks of grey.

Hark! proudly hark! with that true tone
They welcomed him to land and throne;
So ere they die they fain would ring
The jubilee of England's king.

Hearts of old Cornwall, fare ye well!
Fast fade such scenes from field and dell;
How wilt thou lack, my own dear land,
Those trusty arms, that faithful band!

"The ancient spirit is not dead,
Old times methinks are breathing here,"
was my very natural thought on a recent visit to the school and church of this parish; wherein I found "whatsoever things are true, whatsoever things are pure, whatsoever things are lovely, whatsoever things are of good report," most nobly and vigorously upheld by the young Vicar, the Rev. W. K. Buck.—[Note in *Ecclesia*, printed 1840.]

[Printed originally in the Second Series of *Records of the Western Shore*, 1836, but assigned in error by Mr. Godwin, to the year 1841.—ED.]

THE KISS OF JUDAS.

HAIL! Master mine!—so did the viper hiss,
   When, with false fang and stealthy crawl, he came
And scorched Messiah's cheek with that vile kiss
He deemed would sojourn there—a brand of shame.

Ah, no! not long!—for soon, and face to face
With his world-shouldering Cross, Lord Jesu stood.
All hail! He said; and, with a proud embrace,
Fastened the traitor's kiss to that forgiving wood!

1841.

THE LOST SHIP: "THE PRESIDENT."

She sailed from New York for England on the 11th of March, 1841, with many passengers, among whom were Lord William Lennox and Tyrone Power, the Comedian, and was never heard of more.

SPEAK! for thou hast a voice, perpetual sea!
    Lift up thy surges with some signal-word:
Show where the pilgrims of the waters be,
    For whom a nation's thrilling heart is stirred.

They went down to thy waves with joyous pride,
    They trod with steadfast feet thy billowy way:
The eyes of wondering men beheld them glide
    Swift in the arrowy distance: where are they?

Didst thou arise upon that giant frame,
    Mad, that the strength of man with thee should strive?
And proud, thy rival element to tame,
    Didst swallow them in conscious depths, alive?

Or, shorn and powerless, hast thou bade them lie,
    Their stately ship, a carcase of the foam:
Where still they watch the ocean and the sky,
    And fondly dream that they have yet a home?

If thou hast drawn them, mighty tide! declare,
    To some far-off immeasurable plain,
'Mid all things wild and wonderful, and where
    The magnet woos her iron mate in vain.

Doth hope still soothe their souls, or gladness thrill?
  Is peace amid those wanderers of the foam?
Say! is the old affection yearning still,
  With all the blessèd memories of home?

Or, is it over—life, and breath, and thought,
  The living feature, and the breathing form?
Is the strong man become a thing of nought,
  And the red blood of rank no longer warm?

Thou answerest not—thou stern and haughty sea!
  There is no sound in earth, or wave, or air.
Roll on, ye tears! Oh, what shall solace be
  To hearts that pant for hope, but breathe despair?

Nay, mourner! there is sunlight o'er the deep—
  A gentle rainbow on the darkling cloud:
A voice more mighty than the storms shall sweep
  The shore of tempests when the storm is loud.

What though they woke the whirlwinds of the West,
  Or roused the tempest from some Eastern lair?
Or clave the cloud with thunder in its breast?
  Lord of the awful waters! Thou wert there!

All-Merciful! the day, the doom were Thine:
  Thou didst surround them on the seething sea;
Thy love too deep, Thy mercy too divine,
  To quench them in an hour unmeet for Thee.

If winds were mighty, Thou wert in the gale!
  If their feet failed them, in Thy midst they trod!
Storms could not urge the bark, or force the sail,
  Or rend the quivering helm—away from God.

May, 1841.

[Published in *Reeds Shaken with the Wind,* 1843. Reprinted in *The Cornish Ballads.*]

THE FIRST PRINCE OF WALES.

A.D. 1284.

At the death of Llewellyn, the Welsh demanded a native Prince: so King Edward I. of England, who was then in Wales, sent for Eleanor his Queen, and she, soon after her arrival at Caernarvon Castle, was delivered of a son whom the King presented to the Welsh chieftains, and whom they acknowledged as their native Prince.

LLWYD.

"WEEP, noble lady, weep no more,
  The woman's joy is won:
Fear not! thy time of grief is o'er,
  And thou hast borne a son."

Then ceased the Queen from pain and cry,
  And as she sweetly smiled,
The tears stood still within her eye,
  The mother saw her child.

" Now bear him to the castle-gate:"
  Thus did the King command;
There, stern and stately all, they wait,
  The warriors of the land.

H—2

They met—another lord to claim—
    And loud their voices rung:
"We will not brook the stranger's name,
    Nor serve a Saxon tongue."

"Our king shall breathe a British birth,
    And speak with native voice;
He shall be famous in the earth,
    The chieftain of our choice."

Then might you hear the drawbridge fall,
    And echoing footsteps nigh;
And hearken! by yon haughty wall
    A low and infant cry,

"God save your Prince!" King Edward said;
    "Your wayward wish is won:
Behold him from his mother's bed,
    My child—my firstborn son!"

"Here in his own, his native place,
    His future feet shall stand,
And rule the children of your race
    In language of the land."

'Twas strange to see; so sternly smiled
    Those warriors grey and grim.
How little thought King Edward's child
    Who thus would welcome him!

Nor knew they then how proud the tone
    They taught their native vales;
The sound whole nations lived to own—
    "God save the Prince of Wales!"

1841.

THE FIGURE-HEAD OF THE CALEDONIA AT HER CAPTAIN'S GRAVE.

WE laid them in their lowly rest,
    The strangers of a distant shore;
We smoothed the green turf on their breast,
    'Mid baffled Ocean's angry roar;
And there, the relique of the storm,
We fixed fair Scotland's figured form.

She watches by her bold, her brave,
    Her shield towards the fatal sea:
Their cherished lady of the wave
    Is guardian of their memory.
Stern is her look, but calm, for there
No gale can rend or billow bear.

Stand, silent image! stately stand,
    Where sighs shall breathe and tears be shed,
And many a heart of Cornish land,
    Will soften for the stranger dead.
They came in paths of storm; they found
This quiet home in Christian ground.

1841.

QUEEN GUENNIVAR'S ROUND.

NAIAD for Grecian waters!
   Nymph for the fountain-side!
But old Cornwall's bounding daughters
   For grey Dundagel's tide.

The wild wind proudly gathers
   Round the ladies of the land;
And the blue wave of their fathers
   Is joyful where they stand.

Naiad for Grecian waters!
   Nymph for the fountain-side!
But old Cornwall's bounding daughters
   For grey Dundagel's tide.

Yes! when memory rejoices
   In her long belovèd theme,
Fair forms and thrilling voices
   Will mingle with my dream.

Naiad for Grecian waters!
   Nymph for the fountain-side
But old Cornwall's bounding daughters
   For grey Dundagel's tide.

[Published in *All the Year Round*, 1841, and in *The Cornish Ballads*, 1869].

ISHA CHERIOTH.

THEY say his sin was dark and deep,
   Men shudder at his name—
They spurn at me because I weep,
   They call my sorrow, shame.

I know not! I remember well
   Our city's native street,
The path—the olive trees—the dell
   Where Cherioth's daughters meet:

And there, where clustering vineyards rest,
   And palms look forth above,
He kindled in my maiden-breast
   The glory of his love!

He left me—but with holier thought,
   Bound for a mightier scene;
In proud Capernaum's path he sought
   The noble Nazarene!

They tell of treachery bought and sold—
   Perchance their words be truth—
I only see the scenes of old;
   I hear his voice in youth.

And I sit, as Rizpah sate,
   Where life and hope are fled,
I sought him not in happier state,
   I will not leave my dead!

No! I must weep, though all around
    Be hatred and despair;
One sigh shall soothe this fatal ground,
    A Cherioth maiden's prayer!

[From *Ecclesia*, 1840.]

A BALLAD FOR A COTTAGE WALL.

"Thou shalt fasten them upon the lintels of thy doors."

A CHILD sate by the meadow-gate,
    A tender girl and young;
With many a tear her eyes were wet,
    And thus she sate and sung:—

"Ah! woe is me! for I have no grace,
    Nor goodness as I ought;
I never shall go to the happy place,
    And 'tis all my parents' fault.

"To this bad world they brought me in,
    A place where all must grieve;
With flesh of misery and sin,
    From Adam and from Eve.

"And then they shunned the churchyard path,
    Where holy angels haunt;
They would not bear their child of wrath
    To yonder blessèd font.

" They kept me from that second birth,
    Which God to baptism gave;
And now I have no hope on earth,
    Nor peace beyond the grave.

" Yet a thought is in my mind to-day—
    It came I know not how:
I will go to the font at church, and say
    I seek my baptism now.

" Yes! God is kind: I shall then have grace
    And goodness as I ought.
For oh! if I lose the happy place
    'Twill be my poor parents' fault."

'Twas a child of meek and gentle kind,
    A tender girl and young;
And angels put into her mind
    The solemn words she sung.

[Printed in *Reeds Shaken with the Wind*, 1843, and in *Echoes from Old Cornwall*, 1846, as "A Baptismal Ballad." Probably issued as a leaflet, or broadside ballad, *circa* 1841.—ED.]

A LEGEND OF THE HIVE.

BEHOLD those wingèd images,
    Bound for their evening bowers:
They are the nation of the bees,
    Born from the breath of flowers.
Strange people they! a mystic race,
In life, in food, and dwelling-place.

A LEGEND OF THE HIVE.

They first were seen on earth, 'tis said,
    When the rose breathes in spring:
Men thought her blushing bosom shed
    These children of the wing.
But lo! their hosts went down the wind,
Filled with the thoughts of God's own mind.

They built them houses made with hands,
    And there alone they dwell:
No man to this day understands
    The mystery of their cell.
Your mighty sages cannot see
The deep foundations of the bee.

Low in the violets' breast of blue,
    For treasured food they sink;
They know the flowers that hold the dew,
    For their small race to drink.
They glide—King Solomon might gaze
With wonder on their awful ways.

And once—it is a grandame's tale,
    Yet filled with secret lore—
There dwelt within a woodland vale,
    Fast by old Cornwall's shore,
An ancient woman, worn and bent,
Fallen nature's mournful monument.

A home had they, the clustering race,
    Beside her garden wall:
All blossoms breathed around the place,
    And sunbeams fain would fall.

The lily loved that combe the best
Of all the valleys of the west.

But so it was, that on a day
   When summer built her bowers,
The waxen wanderers ceased to play
   Around the cottage flowers.
No hum was heard, no wing would roam:
They dwelt within their cloister'd home.

This lasted long—no tongue could tell
   Their pastime or their toil;
What binds the soldier to his cell?
   Who should divide the spoil?
It lasted long—it fain would last,
Till autumn rustled on the blast.

Then sternly went that woman old,
   She sought the chancel floor,
And there, with purpose bad and bold,
   Knelt down amid the poor.
She took—she hid—that blessèd bread,
Whereon the Invisible is shed.

She bore it to her distant home,
   She laid it by the hive:
To lure the wanderers forth to roam,
   That so her store might thrive.
'Twas a wild wish, a thought unblest,
Some evil legend of the west.

But lo! at morning tide, a sign
  For wondering eyes to trace:
They found above that bread, a shrine
  Reared by the harmless race.
They brought their walls from bud and flower,
They built bright roof and beamy tower.

Was it a dream? or did they hear,
  Float from those golden cells,
A sound as of some psaltery near,
  Or soft and silvery bells;
A low sweet psalm that grieved within,
In mournful memory of the sin.

Was it a dream? 'tis sweet no less:
  Set not the vision free,
Long let the lingering legend bless
  The nation of the bee.
So shall they bear upon their wings
A parable of sacred things.

So shall they teach, when men blaspheme
  Or sacrament or shrine,
That humbler things may fondly dream
  Of mysteries divine;
And holier hearts than his may beat
Beneath the bold blasphemer's feet.

[From *Reeds Shaken by the Wind, The Second Cluster*, 1844; printed also in *Echoes from Old Cornwall*, 1846. In Mr. Godwin's collection, the last line of the ninth stanza is altered to
  "That is what Jesu, Master said!"
The thought, however, as it stands, is clearly the same as that which occurs in Mr. Hawker's note to "Ephphatha" (p. 75, *infra*.—ED.]

GENOVEVA.

Part the First.

MORNING.

NOW hearken, lords and ladies gay,
    And ye shall understand
The wonders of a legend-lay,
    From the old German land!
She, of my song, in Eden's bowers,
    A sainted lady lies;
And wears a chaplet of the flowers
    That grow in Paradise.

Her father gloried in her birth,
    That daughter of his fame;
The sweetest sound he knew on earth
    Was Genoveva's name.
She dwelt, a fair and holy child,
    Beside her mother's knee:
She grew, a maiden meek and mild,
    And pure as pure could be.

And so it was, that when the maid
    Fulfilled her childhood's vow,
Saint Hildorf's lifted hands were laid
    Upon no lovelier brow.
And said they, as along the aisle
    The lords and ladies poured,
" How will she gladden with her smile
    The castle of her lord!"

Right soon a stately champion came
    For that bright damsel's hand;
The sound of County Siegfried's fame
    Was sung in many a land.
He came, he knelt, he woo'd, he won,
    As warriors win the bride;
Duke Pfalz hath hailed him as his son,
    At Genoveva's side.

Then might you hear the matin-bell,
    With echoes low and sweet,
Where at Saint Hildorf's sacred cell
    The youth and maiden meet.
And hark! they plight the mystic vow,
    The troth that time shall try,
When years have worn the beamy brow,
    And quenched the laughing eye.

Now turn we to the castle gate,
    Wreathed with the peaceful vine,
Where County Siegfried holds his state,
    Beside the Rhine! the Rhine!
They bring white blossoms from the bowers,
    The rose-leaves hide the ground;
Ah! gentle dame, beneath the flowers
    The coiling worm is found!

Yet day by day went bounding on,
    Nor would the warrior roam:
The brightness of his lady shone
    Throughout Lord Siegfried's home.

She was the garland of his days,
   His blessing and his fame:
His happy hearth hath won the praise
   Of Genoveva's name.

But hark! that stern and sudden sound,
   Along the castle wall:
It shook the echo from the ground,
   That startling trumpet-call.
"To arms! To horse! The Moor! The Moor!
   His pagan banners fly:
The Spaniard and the Frank implore
   Thy German chivalry."

Then might you see, at break of day,
   The stately Siegfried stand:
Harnessed, and in his old array,
   His good sword in his hand.
"And fare-thee-well!" the soldier said,
   "My lady bright and dear:"
He spake, and bent his haughty head,
   To hide a warrior's tear.

"Farewell! and thou my castellain,
   My liege-man true and tried,
Shield, till thy lord shall turn again,
   My lady and my bride.
And ye, good Saints, with unseen eyes,
   Watch her in solemn care;
An angel well might leave the skies
   At Genoveva's prayer."

Part the Second.

EVENING.

AH! woe is me! and well-a-day!
   What scenes of sorrow rise;
And hark! the music of my lay
   Must breathe the breath of sighs.
That guardian—he of trusty fame,
   He seeks a deed abhorred;
He woos to sorrow and to shame,
   The lady of his lord.

But she, fair Genoveva, stands,
   A pure and peerless bride;
Her angel lifts his sheltering hands,
   For ever at her side.
She kneels, she breathes some simple verse,
   Taught by her mother's care;
And the good Saints in Heaven rehearse
   The gentle lady's prayer.

Yet strife and anguish lasted long.
   Till he—that fiendish man,
The anger of his sin was strong,
   And thus his fury ran:—
"Bind ye this foul and wanton dame,
   False to my master's bed;
Hide in the earth both sin and shame,
   Her blood be on her head."

They took the stern command he gave,
   Two vassals fierce and rude;
They bare her to a nameless grave,
   Far in a distant wood.
There knelt she down and meekly prayed,
   In language soft and mild:
"I bear beneath my breast," she said,
   "Your lord, Count Siegfried's child.

"Then let me tarry but awhile,
   Far, far, from earthly eye,
That I may see my infant smile,
   And lay me down and die.
Nay, spare me, in sweet Mary's name,
   Who stood by Jesu's cross;
He from a mother's bosom came,
   That He might die for us."

They melted at the voice they heard,
   They left her lonely there!
The holy angels helped her word—
   There is such force in prayer.
Then wandered she, where that wild wood
   A tangled pathway gave,
Till, lo! in secret solitude,
   A deep and mossy cave.

A source of quiet waters shone
   Along a shadowy glade;
And branches, fair to look upon,
   A dreamy shelter gave.

Her eyes are closed, but not to sleep;
    She bends, but not to pray;
Thrilled with the throes that mothers weep,
    The lonely lady lay.

She sees—what is it nestling near?
    A soft, fair form is nigh:
She hears—sweet Lord, what doth she hear?
    A low and infant cry.
It is her son! her son! the child,
    The first-born of her vow:
See, in his face his father smiled,
    He bears Lord Siegfried's brow.

Good angels! 'twas a sight to see
    That cavern dark and wild;
The nameless stream—the silent tree,
    The mother and her child.
And hark! he weeps—that voice of tears
    Proclaims a child of earth;
O, what shall soothe for holier years
    The sorrow of his birth!

There was no font, no sacred shrine,
    No servant of the Lord;
The waters of the mystic sign
    A mother's hand hath poured.
She breathed on him a word of woes,
    His life in tears begun;
The name a Hebrew mother chose,
    Ben-oni—Sorrow's son.

But ah! what miseries betide
   A mother and her pains!
Her child must die, for famine dried
   The fountain of her veins.
She saw the anguish of his face,
   She heard his bitter cry,
And went forth from that woeful place,
   She could not see him die.

Yet still, again, her feet must turn
   Back to that cavern wild:
Yea! even in death, she fain would yearn
   Once more upon her child.
What doth she see? A fair young doe
   A mother's task hath done,
Bent at his side: her milk must flow
   To soothe the lady's son.

She wept—she wept, she could no less,
   Tears sweet and grateful ran;
The mute thing of the wilderness
   Hath softer heart than man.
She came, that wild deer of the herd,
   Moved by some strange control,
There was a mystic touch that stirred
   The yearnings of her soul.

And there they dwelt, the gentle three—
   In peace, if not in joy,
Until he stood beside her knee,
   A fair and thoughtful boy.

The doe, the lady, and the youth,
    Seven long and weary years,
Their calm and patient life; in sooth
    It was a sight for tears.

She fed him with the forest fruits
    That summer branches gave;
She gathered wild and wholesome roots,
    To cheer their wintry cave:
They drank from that fair fountain's bed
    Whose faithful waters run
Bright as when first his name they shed,
    Ben-oni—Sorrow's son.

And she hath framed, with chosen boughs,
    A simple cross of wood;
And taught the lad his childhood's vows,
    To Jesu, mild and good.
He learned the legend of the Cross,
    How Mary's blessèd Son
Came down from heaven to die for us,
    And peace and pardon won.

He heard that shadowy angels roam
    Along the woodland dell,
To lead the blessèd to a home
    Where saints and martyrs dwell.
So, when the lady wept and prayed,
    He soothed her secret sighs:
"Sweet mother, let us die," he said,
    "And rest in Paradise."

"Alas! my son, my tender son,
  What wilt thou do," she sighed,
"When I thy mother shall be gone?—
  Thou hast no friend beside.
There is thy Sire of Heavenly birth,
  His love is strong and sure:
But he, thy father of the earth,
  He spurns thee from his door."

"Nay, tell me, mother dear," he said,
  "I pray thee tell to me,
Are they not, all men, gone and dead,
  Except thy son and thee?"
"Ah! no, there be, my gentle child,
  Whole multitudes afar;
Yet is it happier in this wild,
  Than where their dwellings are.

"They cast me out to woe and shame,
  Here in this den to hide:
They blighted Genoveva's name,
  Lord Siegfried's chosen bride.
But soon the weary will have rest,
  I breathe with failing breath;
There is within thy mother's breast,
  The bitterness of death."

"Then, mother kind, in thy dark grave,
  Alone, thou shalt not lie:
Before our Cross, here in this grave,
  Together let us die.

Yea, let me look on no man's face,
    Since such stern hearts there be:
But here, in this our lonely place,
    Here will I die with thee."

"Ah! noble heart! thy words are sooth
    I breathe their sound again:
Better to pass away in youth,
    Than live with bearded men."
And thou! the Lady of his birth,
    Farewell! a calm farewell!
Thou wert not meant for this vile earth,
    But with the saints to dwell.

PART THE THIRD.

ANOTHER DAY.

Mark ye, how spear and helmet glare,
    And red-cross banners shine,
While thrilling trumpets cleave the air
    Along the Rhine! the Rhine!
Count Siegfried from the wars is come,
    And gathering vassals wait
To welcome the stern warrior home
    To his own castle gate.

But where is she, his joy, his pride,
    The garland of his fame?
Away! away! her image hide,
    He cannot brook her name.

Yet soon the whispered words are breathed,
   And faithful lips declare
How a vile serpent's folds were wreathed
   Around their lady fair.

They tell his vassal's treacherous crime,
   The bow his malice bent,
Till Genoveva, in her prime,
   Had perished, innocent.
Alas! what torrent tears must roll
   In fierce and angry shower!
O! what shall soothe Count Siegfried's soul
   In that o'erwhelming hour?

He hides him in some vaulted room,
   Far from the light of day;
He will not look on beauty's bloom,
   Nor hear the minstrel's lay.
They try him with the trumpet sound
   On many an echoing morn;
They tempt him forth with hawk and hound,
   And breathe the hunter's horn.

They loose the gazehound from the chain,
   They bring both steed and spear,
Lord Siegfried's hand must rule the rein,
   And rouse the ruddy deer.
On! through the wild, the war-horse bounds
   Beneath his stately form,
He charges 'mid those rushing hounds
   With footsteps like the storm.

"Down! Donner, down! hold, Hubert, hold!"
  What is yon sight of fear?
A strange wild youth, a maiden bold
  That guard yon panting deer!"
A fleecy skin was folded round
  Her breast, with woman's pride,
And some dead fawn the youth hath found,
  He wears its dappled hide.

"Who? whence are ye?" the warrior said,
  "That haunt this secret cave?
Ha! is it so? and do the dead
  Come from their hollow grave?"
"I live, I breathe the breath of life,
  No evil have I done;
I am thy true, thy chosen wife,
  And this is Siegfried's son!"

He stood, as severed souls may stand
  At first, when forth they fare,
And shadowy forms—a stranger-band—
  Will greet them in the air.
He bounds, he binds her to his heart,
  His own, his rescued bride:
No more! O! never more to part,
  E'en death shall not divide.

See now, they move along the wild,
  With solemn feet and slow,
The warrior and his graceful child,
  The lady and the doe.

They stand before the castle-gate,
   Rich with the clustering vine,
Again shall Siegfried hold his state,
   Beside the Rhine ! the Rhine !

They come, they haste from many a land,
   For fast the tidings spread,
And there doth Genoveva stand,
   Bright as the arisen dead.
Her mother weeps, by God's dear grace,
   Glad tears are in her eye ;
Duke Pfalz has seen his daughter's face,
   And now—now let him die.

Yea, from his calm and distant cell
   The sainted Hildorf came,
His spirit bowed beneath the spell
   Of Genoveva's name.
He came, he sought that solemn cave,
   The lady's patient home,
He measured it with aisle and nave,
   He shaped a shadowy dome.

He knelt in votive solitude,
   He fixed both saint and sign,
And bade them build, in that lone wood,
   A fair and stately shrine.
There might you read for many an age,
   In the rich window's ray,
Traced, as along some pictured page,
   The legend of my lay.

The image of their youth was there,
    The bridegroom and the bride;
The porch, where Genoveva fair
    Knelt at her Siegfried's side.
There, through the storied glass, the scene
    In molten beauty falls,
When she, with mild and matron mien,
    Shone in her husband's halls.

There was the cave, the wood, the stream,
    In radiance soft and warm,
And evermore the noon-day beam
    Came through some angel's form.
The youth was shown in that wild dress,
    His mother's cross he bare;
Saint John in the old wilderness
    Was not more strangely fair.

But where they breathe their holiest vows,
    And eastern sunbeams fall,
A simple cross, of woodland boughs,
    Stands by the chancel wall.
It is the lady's lonely sign,
    By mournful fingers made,
That self-same symbol decks the shrine
    That soothed the cavern's shade.

Behind yon altar, reared on high,
    A lady breathes in stone;
A sculptured deer is crouching nigh,
    An infant weeps alone.

A word is there, but not of woe,
  One voice, a prayer to claim,
Beneath the lady and the doe
  Is Genobeba's name.

Thus lived, thus loved she, and she died,
  But old, and full of days;
Ask ye how time and truth have tried
  The legend of her praise?
She of my song, in Eden's bowers
  A sainted lady lies,
And wears a garland of the flowers
  That grow in Paradise.

1842.
[This Poem first appeared in *German Ballads, Songs*, &c., edited by Miss Smedley, and published, without date, by James Burns; also in *Reeds Shaken with the Wind; The Second Cluster.* 1844, and in *Echoes from Old Cornwall*, 1846.—ED.]

THE LADY'S WELL.

IT flowed—like Light from the voice of God,
  Silent, and calm, and fair;
It shone where the child and the parent trod,
  In the soft and evening air.

"Look at that spring, my father dear,
  Where the white blossoms fell:
Why is it always bright and clear?
  And why the Lady's Well?"

"Once on a time, my own dear child,
  There dwelt across the sea
A lovely Mother, meek and mild,
  From blame and blemish free.

"And Mary was her blessèd name,
  Though not by men ador'd:
Its sound some thoughts of love should claim
  From all who love their Lord.

"A Child was hers—a Heavenly birth,
  As pure as pure could be:
He had no father of the earth,
  The Son of God was He.

"He came down to her from above,
  He died upon the Cross:
We never can do for Him, my love,
  What He hath done for us.

"And so to make His praise endure,
  Because of Jesu's fame,
Our fathers called things bright and pure
  By His fair Mother's name.

"*She* is the Lady of the Well,
  Her memory was meant
With lily and with rose to dwell,
  By waters innocent."

[Printed, as it stands above, in *Ecclesia*, 1840. Designated "A Reprint" in *Reeds Shaken with the Wind*, 1843. Reprinted also in *Echoes from Old Cornwall*, 1846. In later editions, material alterations have been made; *e.g.* the fourth verse is made to read thus:—

"And Mary was her blessèd name,
  In every land adored:
Its very sound deep love should claim
  From all who love their Lord."

Mr. Godwin has wrongly assigned to it the date 1842, and prints the altered verse.—ED.]

WORDS BY THE WATERS.

"Thou shalt remember the days of darkness: for they are many."
Eccles.

WHY dost thou wait and watch the gloomy shore,
Where the rocks darken and the surges roar,—
While down the steep the foamy cataract raves,
And rolls dissolved amid the wilderness of waves?

Lift up thine eyes along the distant tide,
Where the glad waters glisten as they glide:
The ocean-plains! how beautiful they be—
Lo! Heaven itself comes down to sojourn on the sea!

Ah, no! for thoughts like mine—too softly bright—
That scene is touched with all too gentle light;
Fair visions haunt those waves—sweet dreams arise—
And billows bathed in glory, bound to meet the skies!

Gloom, gloom! for me—the mountain clothed in cloud,
The shore of tempests when the storm is loud,
Where wild winds rush, and broken waters roll,
And all is dark and stern, like my own wintry soul!

What have I, silvery scene, to do with thee?
Mirror of Heaven! thou glad and glorious sea,
Thou dost but mock thy wave-worn wanderer's gaze
With that smooth prophecy of far-off lovelier days!
1842.

THE TWAIN.[1]

𝔚𝔥𝔦𝔠𝔥 𝔬𝔫𝔩𝔶 𝔥𝔞𝔱𝔥 𝔍𝔪𝔪𝔬𝔯𝔱𝔞𝔩𝔦𝔱𝔶.

TWO sunny children wandered, hand in hand,
    By the blue waves of far Gennesaret,
For there their Syrian father drew the net,
With multitudes of fishes, to the land.
    One was the twin, even he whose blessèd name
    Hath in ten thousand shrines this day a fame—
Thomas the Apostle, one of the ethereal band.
    But he, his Hebrew brother, who can trace
    His name, the city where he dwelt, his place,
Or grave? We know not, none may understand.
    There were two brethren in the field: the one
    Shall have no memory underneath the sun;
The other shines, beacon of many a strand,
A star upon the brow of night, here in the rocky land.

---

[1] "I inserted in my sermon an account of the discovery of St. Thomas the Apostle's death and burial in India. Thus the sole question ever was, Is it apostolic? Then it must endure. Was it from one of the Twelve? Then it will never pass away. A small company of Christian men found in Upper India among the mountains, origin unknown; afterwards a tomb, with a staff and cross, a legend that there lived, laboured, and was slain, St. Thomas the Apostle. St. Thomas the Twain, even in his ashes, survived the apostolic fire, and whole ages after he was dust virtue went out of the dust of St. Thomas of India."—*Letter from Mr. Hawker, dated June* 15, 1856.

[First printed in *Reeds Shaken with the Wind*, 1844.]

THE NIGHT COMETH.

WHEN darkness fills the western sky,
And sleep, the twin of death, is nigh,
What soothes the soul at set of sun?
The pleasant thought of duty done.

Yet must the pastoral slumbers be
The shepherd's by the eastern tree,
Broken and brief—with dreams that tell
Of ravaged flock and poisoned well!

Be still, my soul! fast wears the night—
Soon shall day dawn in holier light:
Old faces—ancient hearts—be there,
And well known voices thrill the air!

The Festival of St. Andrew, 1842.

[The date stands thus in Mr. Godwin's collection; but the poem was written at least six years earlier, having been printed in the Second Series of *Records of the Western Shore,* 1836.—ED.]

THE DIRGE.

"The first line of these verses haunted the memory and the lips of a good and blameless young farmer who died in my parish some years ago. It was, as I conceive, a fragment of some forgotten dirge, of which he could remember no more. But it was his strong desire that "the words" should be "put upon his headstone," and he wished me also to write "some other words, to make it complete." I fulfilled his entreaty, and the stranger who visits my churchyard will find this dirge carven in stone, "in sweet remembrance of the just," and to the praise of the dead, Richard Cann, whose soul was carried by the angels into Paradise on the 15th of February, 1842."

"SING from the chamber to the grave!"
 Thus did the dead man say:
"A sound of melody I crave,
 Upon my burial-day.

"Bring forth some tuneful instrument,
 And let your voices rise:
My spirit listened, as it went,
 To music of the skies.

"Sing sweetly while you travel on,
 And keep the funeral slow:—
The angels sing where I am gone,
 And you should sing below.

"Sing from the threshold to the porch,
 Until you hear the bell;
And sing you loudly in the church,
 The Psalms I love so well.

A THOUGHT AT MATINS.

"Then bear me gently to my grave,
    And as you pass along,
Remember, 'twas my wish to have
    A pleasant funeral song.

"So earth to earth, and dust to dust!
    And though my flesh decay,
My soul shall sing among the just
    Until the Judgment-day."

1842.

[Published, but without the above comment, in *Reeds Shaken with the Wind*, 1843, as "A Cornish Death-Song;" then with the same title in *Echoes of Old Cornwall*, 1846; and again in *Footsteps of Former Men in Far Cornwall*, 1870.—ED.]

A THOUGHT AT MATINS.

SEPTEMBER 18, 1842.

THE sun fell fair on Kelly walls
    On Maitland's christening-day,
And lighted up his father's halls
    With autumn's loveliest ray:
The Angel of his Baptism trod
A path bright from the home of God!

Shall it not be to us a sign —
  A parable of joy—
That radiance from above will shine
  Around our gentle boy?
Since such the sun that greets his gaze,
This first-born of his Christian-days!

KELLY HOUSE.
  September, 1842.

[From *Reeds Shaken with the Wind*, 1843.]

THE BAPTISM OF THE PEASANT AND THE PRINCE.

"Every one that is perfect shall be as His Master."—
ST. LUKE vi. 40.

I CLIMBED a poor and narrow stair,
  The prince's christening day;
I sought a cottage bed, for there
  A travail'd woman lay.

With covering thin, and scanty vest,
  Her babe was on her arm:
It was the strong love in her breast
  That kept that infant warm.

I came, a country minister,
  A servant of the Lord;
To bless that mother's child for her,
  With Water and the Word.

The dim light struggling o'er the room
   Scarce reached the lowly bed :
And thus 'mid woe, and want, and gloom,
   The Sacrament was shed.

Then said I—for the woman smiled
   As she took back her son—
" Be glad ! for lo ! that little child,
   Is 'mong God's children, one.

" Henceforth it hath a name on high,
   Where blessèd angels shine :
Nay, one will leave his native sky,
   To watch this babe of thine.

" Be glad ! this very day they meet,
   In a far loftier scene,
With blessing and with vow to greet
   The offspring of a Queen.

" Bright faces beam in bannered halls,
   Around the noble boy :
And princes teach the echoing walls
   The glory of their joy.

" Yet will the self-same words be said,
   Our lips have utter'd now ;
And water, such as here we shed,
   Must bless that princely brow.

" One Cross the twain shall seal and sign,
   An equal grace be poured :
One Faith, one Church, one Heaven, will join
   The labourer and his lord."

"Thanks be to God!" in language mild,
   The humble woman said:
"Who sends such kindness to my child,
   Here in its mother's bed:

"And bless our Queen with health and grace,
   Her's is a happy reign:
O! one smile of her baby's face
   Pays her for all her pain."[1]

January 25, 1842.

[1] St. John xvii.

[Printed in *Reeds Shaken with the Wind*, 1843, and in *Echoes from Old Cornwall*, 1846.]

THE WOLF.

LONG centuries agone—this very day,
   In a far wilderness of Syrian sand,
 Urging his steed amid an armèd band,
The wolf of Benjamin was on the prey.
   But lo! a light, a voice, a thrilling sound,
   And where was Saul of Tarsus? Sternly bound,
A fettered thrall, in darkness there he lay!
   Shall he arise and conquer? can he toil
   Once more in war and yet divide the spoil?
For thus dim Jacob traced the wanderer's way.

Answer, proud Corinth! stern and stately Rome,
Soft Ephesus, and thou, the populous home
Of many a city, old Galatia! say,—
Did not the warrior win and wear a conqueror's array?

The Festival of St. Paul, 1843.

[First printed in *Reeds Shaken with the Wind*, 1844.]

HYMN FOR HOLY INNOCENTS' DAY.

ALL hail! ye Martyr Flowers,
    Born with the blush of day,
Blossoms for Eden's bowers,
    To grace Lord Jesu's way!

Young firstlings for the shrine,
    Lambs of a tender fold,
Around the altar shine,
    And palmy garlands hold.

Thee, Jesu! let us laud,
    Child of a mother's love.
With Him the Father, God,
    And that Eternal Dove.

1843.

[From Mr. Hawker's MSS., and not until now included in any collection of his *Poems*. It may have been printed as a leaflet for local distribution, but we have not seen it in that form.—ED.]

THE WELL OF ST. JOHN.

"The well of St. John in the Wilderness stands and flows softly in the eastern boundary of Morwenstow Glebe. In the old Latin Endowment, still preserved in Bishop Brentingham's Register in the Archives of Exeter, A.D. 1296, the Church land is said to extend eastward, *ad quendam fontem Johannis*. Water wherewithal to fill the font for baptism is always drawn from this well by the Sacristan in pitchers set apart for this purpose."

THEY dreamed not in old Hebron, when the sound
    Went through the city, that the promised son
    Was born to Zachary, and his name was John;
They little thought, that here in this far ground,
    Beside the Severn sea, that Hebrew child
    Would be a cherished memory of the wild;
Here, where the pulses of the ocean bound
    Whole centuries away, while one meek cell,
    Built by the fathers o'er a lonely well,
Still breathes the Baptist's sweet remembrance round.
    A spring of silent waters with his name,
    That from the angel's voice in music came,
Here in the wilderness so faithful found,
It freshens to this day the Levite's grassy mound.

    The Festival of St. John the Baptizer, 1843.

[From *Echoes from Old Cornwall*; reprinted in *Cornish Ballads*.]

THE OBLATION.

A WEB of woven wool, fringed all around,
    Ruddy and rich in hue, like Syrian wine;
With golden leaves inlaid on that dark ground,
    That seemed just shed from some o'ershadowing vine:
    Such was the lady's offering at Morwenna's shrine.

We laid it on the altar, while the word
    Lingered in echoes o'er the unconscious wall;
The voice that prophesied our God had heard
    The sound of alms, and would remember all;
    'Twas the Child Jesu's day, the Bethlehem Festival.

We *offer'd it* to Him :—scorn not the phrase
    Ye proud and stately magnates of the land;
Grudge not the poor their pence, nor God His praise,
    Though as our simple fathers stood, we stand,
    And render thus our gifts with meek and votive hand.

We left it in that chancel deck'd with flowers,
    And boughs that blossom'd like old Aaron's rod;
For faithful hands had built them leafy bowers
    Along our aisles, such as the angels trod
    When Moses saw the bush, and Abraham talked with God.

Christmas Day, 1843.

[From *Reeds Shaken with the Wind, The Second Cluster*, 1844. Reprinted in *Echoes from Old Cornwall*, and in *Cornish Ballads* (wherein it is entitled "The Lady's Offering"). The latter title is adopted also by Mr. Godwin.—ED.]

ABSALOM'S PILLAR.

REAR yonder rock! vast, pillared, and alone,
  Like some grim god revealed in awful stone;
There build my place, and bid my memory stand,
Throned in mid air, to rule along the land.

There hew my name where Judah's daughters glide
To weave their shadowy dance at evening-tide;
Lo! their soft voices thrill the stony shade—
"Here the Prince Absalom, who died in youth, is laid."

I have no son, no daughter of my fame
To breathe, 'mid future hearts, their father's name;
I live with many men, I die alone;
I go into the ground—Rear the surviving stone!

  1844.

A CHRIST-CROSS RHYME.

CHRIST His Cross shall be my speed,
  Teach me, Father John, to read:
That in church on holy day,
  I may chant the psalm and pray.

Let me learn, that I may know
What the shining windows show:
Where the lovely Lady stands,
With that bright Child in her hands.

Teach me letters, A, B, C,
Till that I shall able be
Signs to know and words to frame,
And to spell sweet Jesus' Name.

Then, dear Master, will I look,
Day and night in that fair book,
Where the tales of saints are told,
With their pictures, all in gold.

Teach me, Father John, to say
Vesper-verse and matin-lay:
So when I to God shall plead,
Christ His Cross shall be my speed.

1845.

[First printed in *Willis's Current Notes*, November, 1855, p. 86. Reprinted in *Cornish Ballads*.]

ONE IS NOT.

THERE is a cross in Oxford, built of stone,
    They call it there "The Martyrs' Monument;"
Wise-hearted workmen rear'd it, and they spent
In that proud toil, labour and gold unknown.

There have they pictur'd many a visible thought
And deep device, whereby the fathers wrought
Doctrines in walls, and gave dumb roofs a tone.
 Yet, hearken! in yon cloister dim and old,
 They show a simple casket fram'd to hold
An ancient staff.   Ye walls of stern Saint John!
 Watch well that relic of the days gone by—
 Thereon Laud lean'd when he went forth to die.
Ha! stout old man, thy fame is still our own,
Though banish'd be thy memory from the graven
  stone!

[Printed in *Echoes from Old Cornwall*, 1846, but not included in Mr. Godwin's collection.—ED.]

A VOICE FROM THE PLACE OF ST. MOR-WENNA IN THE ROCKY LAND;

UTTERED

TO THE SISTERS OF MERCY AT THE TAMAR MOUTH.

PAUSE, Pilgrim! where our Severn sea
 Rolls its stern waters, wild and free,
And mark, above yon chancel-side,
The Cross! whereon Lord Jesu died!
What memories meet—what visions blend,
On that dear Death-bed of a Friend!

The Priest of Baldiu traced the sign
With mystic lore and rule and line—

Rodolph, the Lord of Clinton,[1] gave
That wall that looks along the wave,
And stately Cross to breathe in stone
Mount Calvary's deed to days unknown.

And be there men, dull, hard, and stern,
Who from that sight can coldly turn?
And, like some loathsome shape, would hide
The last couch of the Crucified?
The latest thing His fingers held
When Heaven was won, and Satan quelled!

Forgive them, tender Lord and true!
Alas! they heed not what they do;
Heaven's light in them is dim and cold,
They know not what Thy saints behold:
They see not as Thine angels see:
Dark Plym! I wail for them and thee!

O City! where my birth-place stands,
How art thou fallen amid the lands!
Thy daughters bold—thy sons unblest—
A withered Salem of the West!
Hark! from yon hill what tones arise—
"Thy peace is hidden from thine eyes!"

Nay! there be forty—twenty—ten
All women true, and trusty men—
A faithful band, like angels given,
To plead the Patriarch's prayer with Heaven;

---

[1] The chancel of Morwenstow has just been nobly restored by the piety of Rodolph, Baron Clinton, and the Lady Elizabeth Georgiana, his wife.

And one, a thrilling Lady, stands,
Whose voice might rescue sentenced lands!

Daughter! my spirit turns to thee:
Here, by the lonely Severn sea,
I, too, have borne, years fierce and long,
All hatred, and rebuke, and wrong:
And now thy truth shall soothe the sigh—
The life I live—the death I die;

For, lo! the Day—the Thrones are near—
And hark! 'mid sounds of hope and fear,
They call, from countries far and wide,
The wood whereon Messias died!
They bear it forth to bless or ban—
The signal of the Son of Man!

How shall men bear, amid their loss,
That Resurrection of the Cross!
The sign they mocked, by angels borne,
The banner of the Eternal Morn!
Once more beside its Lord to stand,
The Trophy Tree of Holy Land!

Up! Prophet-Lady, stern and calm,
Seek not a tent beneath the Palm,
Like Isha Lapidoth [2] the wise:—
As Jael, Heber's wife—arise—
Up! spare not! wield thy noble name!
The Lord hath sold thee foes and fame!

[2] Deborah, wife of Lapidoth, who arose from beneath the Palm, between Ramah and Bethel.

NOTES.

The Forefathers.

THEY rear'd their lodges in the wilderness,
Or built them cells beside the shadowy sea,
And there they dwelt with angels, like a dream!
So they unroll'd the Volume of the Book
And fill'd the fields of the Evangelist
With thoughts as sweet as flowers.

The prophecy of the Resurrection of the Real Cross to be borne by Angels in the Judgment, as the Sign of the Son of Man, was a lovely legend of the first fathers, and beautifully "bodied forth." It would be a noble trophy, and, as they also said, a Memorial Pillar, worthy to stand in Paradise among the trees. They held, too, that every bishop and martyr of the Church would be caught up first to meet the Lord in the air, before the resurrection of the general dead, and so to follow the banner to the judgment, as men who are deemed worthy to "sit on thrones," and "to judge angels and the world," and to wait upon the Lord in that day, "as his ancients gloriously." So aforetime they were laid in the ground—these men of noble name—not in the usual posture of the patient dead, who look towards the Orient to watch for the morning, but with their heads to the east and their faces to the west—for so the path of their Lord will be—in an attitude wherein they will be ready to bound from their biers like soldiers from their sleep, and to gather in immediate array around the Son of Man, to pour forth the buried music of their voices in psalms of thanksgiving, suddenly!

I recommend the slanderers of God's servants, before they again presume to revile the imaged death-bed of the Lord, to read, carefully and thoroughly, the works of Gretser, published in Latin, in seventeen folio volumes, at Ratisbon, 1734-41.

R. S. H.,
Vicar of Morwenstow.

Shrove Tuesday, 1849.

[Issued as a small (sq. 16mo.) pamphlet of 13 pages, during the "Selton Controversy," and intended to strengthen the hands of Miss Sellon, Lady Superior of the Sisters of Mercy at Plymouth. A tolerably exhaustive list of the publications to which this controversy gave rise, will be found in Davidson's *Bibliotheca Devoniensis*.—ED.]

"BE OF GOOD CHEER!"

COME, stand upon the deck, and fish for men!
　　Let down and haul, it is Saint Andrew's Day;
　Take we the allotted side, and watch for prey!
We toil all night for nought!—we cast again:
　　They who are fain a multitude to hold,
　　Break their smooth gear, and not a fish enfold!
The meek and patient catch not: tell me then
　　What is our vision?—what the crafty toil
　　Whereby to win the draught and share the spoil?
It was on such a day—the where and when—
　　Empty the basket—desolate and bare
　　The ship of Galilee—yet, faithful there,
The brethren watch'd the deep with patient ken—
　　Simon and Andrew sate, and calm on board
　　Mended their nets—and waited for the Lord!

　　St. Andrew's Day, 1849.

BAAL ZEPHON.[1]

WAS it the shout of storms that rent the sky?
　　The rush of many a whirlwind from its lair?
Or be the fierce Maozzim[2] loose on high?—
　　The old Gods of the North: the Demons of the Air!

[1] The God of the North.
[2] The Gods of the strongholds. (*Cf.* Dan. xi. 38, 39.)

Those Tartar hills! billowy with writhing men;
    That yelling Euxine! throttled with her dead:
The quivering air, as thick with ghosts as when
    The severed souls of Syrian[3] armies fled!

Ah fatal field! Ah doomed and deadly sea!
    Where be the hosts of God?—that ancient band;
Michael the Prince![4] and Uriel!—where are ye,
    That once did valiantly for English land?

Shun ye the flaunting Crescent's baleful sign;
    The circumcisèd hordes of vile Mahound:
Or is the Red-Cross banner loath to shine
    Where Scythian fiends beset the shuddering ground?

Lords of the vassal air, the lightning-tongue,
    The harnessed fires, with footsteps like the storm!
Where is your vaunt, and what your strength among
    Those riders of the cloud, with battle warm?

Sound the stern signal! summon sea and shore;
    Clothe many a steed with thunder for the war!—
An angel, standing at a cottage door
    To guard a peasant's child, is mightier far!

Oh for the Sigil! or the chanted spell!
    The pentacle that Demons know and dread!—
So should Maozzim flee, with baffled yell,
    And the lulled Euxine smooth its billowy bed.'

[3] (*Cf.* 2 Kings xix. 35.

[4] (*Cf.* Dan. x. 21.)

Arise O Lord ! stretch forth Thy red right hand !
Smite the strong Dragon and his Scythian lair !
God visible ! among the nations stand
And bid the traitor Russ thy banished Name[5]
declare !

1854.

[5] The phrase, " And the Son," in the Nicene Creed, is abjured by the Greek Church, with the doctrine which those words contain.

[In *Willis's Current Notes*, April, 1855, p. 29.]

THE DOOM-WELL OF ST. MADRON.

" PLUNGE thy right hand in St. Madron's spring,
If true to its troth be the palm you bring :
But if a false sigil thy fingers bear,
Lay them the·rather on the burning share."

Loud laughed King Arthur whenas he heard
That solemn friar his boding word :
And blithely he sware as a king he may
" We tryst for St. Madron's at break of day."

" Now horse and hattock, both but and ben,"[1]
Was the cry at Lauds, with Dundagel men ;
And forth they pricked upon Routorr side,[2]
As goodly a raid as a king could ride.

[1] The old phrase for butlery and hall.
[2] Sounded *Rowtor*, the "o" open, as in brow.

THE DOOM-WELL OF ST. MADRON.

Proud Gwennivar rode like a queen of the land,
With page and with squire at her bridle hand;
And the twice six knights of the stony ring,
They girded and guarded their Cornish king.

Then they halted their steeds at St. Madron's cell:
And they stood by the monk of the cloistered well;
"Now off with your gauntlets," King Arthur he cried
"And glory or shame for our Tamar side."

'Twere sooth to sing how Sir Gauvain smiled,
When he grasped the waters so soft and mild;
How Sir Lancelot dashed the glistening spray
O'er the rugged beard of the rough Sir Kay.

Sir Bevis he touched and he found no fear:
'Twas a *bénitée* stoup to Sir Belvidere,
How the fountain flashed o'er King Arthur's Queen
Say, Cornish dames, for ye guess the scene.

"Now rede me my riddle, Sir Mordred, I pray,
My kinsman, mine ancient, my *bien-aimé*;
Now rede me my riddle, and rede it aright,
Art thou traitorous knave or my trusty knight?"

He plunged his right arm in the judgment well,
It bubbled and boiled like a cauldron of hell:
He drew and he lifted his quivering limb,
Ha! Sir Judas, how Madron had sodden him!

L

Now let Uter Pendragon do what he can,
Still the Tamar river will run as it ran:
Let King or let Kaiser be fond or be fell,
Ye may harowe their troth in St. Madron's well.

1851.

[First printed in *Willis's Current Notes*, December, 1855, p. 93. Reprinted in *Cornish Ballads*.]

THE CORNISH BOY IN ITALY.

WILD heart of mine! why art thou cold?
  The Lady land these eyes behold!
Olive valleys—vines on the hill—
Heart in my bosom! why art thou still?

Bright earth is round, rich sky above,
But not the scenes I used to love;
Shining the stream, stately the tree,
Home for fair flowers—but not for me.

Ah! the stern rock! clothed with the cloud,
Nest o' the young storm, wayward and loud,
Where the warm prey bounded to die
And awe hath hushed the hunter's cry!

Home of my spirit! could I but see
One ancient hut and stunted tree,
The dame come forth with looks of care,
And sunset fall on my father's hair!

1852

ARSCOTT OF TETCOTT.

ON the ninth of November, in the year fifty-two,
    Three jolly foxhunters, all sons of true blue,
They rode from Pencarrow, not fearing a wet coat,
To take their diversion with Arscott of Tetcott.[1]

He went to his kennel and took them within:
"On Monday," said Arscott, " our joys shall begin.
Both horses and hounds, how they pant to be gone!
How they'll follow afoot, not forgetting Black John!"[2]

When Monday was come, right early at morn
John Arscott arose, and he took down his horn;
He gave it a flourish so loud, in the hall,
Each heard the glad summons and came at the call.

They heard it with pleasure, but Webb[3] was first dressed,
Resolving to give a cold pig to the rest;

---

[1] This is the venerable name of an ancestor of the present Sir Wm. Molesworth, and of the last of the Western Squires who kept open house and open hand. Many a legend and record of his times and deeds still floats unembodied around the oaks of old Tetcott on the Tamar side.

[2] The last of the Jesters. He lived with the hounds, and ran with the hounds, and rare was the run when Jack was not in at the death. His office it was by many a practical joke to amuse Mr. Arscott's guests; among them swallowing living mice and sparrow-mumbling had frequent place. "There they go." shouted John when the fox was found and the dogs went off in full cry—"there they go, like our madam at home!"

[3] *Webb* was Webb, of Bennetts, in Whitstone—a neighbouring squire.

Bold Bob and The Briton,[4] they hastened down stairs—
It was generally suppos'd they neglected their prayers.

At breakfast they scrambled for butter and toast,
But Webb was impatient that time should be lost;
So old Cheyney was ordered to bring to the door
Both horses and hounds, and away to the moor.

On Monday, says Arscott, as he mounted his nag,
"I look to old Black Cap, for he'll hit the drag!"
The drag it was hit, but they said it was old,
For a drag in the morning could not be so cold.

They prick'd it along to Becket and Thorn,
And there the old dogs they set out, I'll be sworn;
'Twas Ringwood and Rally, with capital scent,
Bold Princess and Madcap—good God! how they
    went!

"How far did they make it? How far went they on?
How far did they make it?" said Simon the Son;[5]
"O'er the moors," said Joe Goodman, "hark to
    Bacchus, the word!"
"Hark to Vulcan," cried Arscott, "that's it, by the
    Lord!"

"Hark to Princess!" says Arscott; "there's a fresh
    Tally-ho!"
The dogs they soon caught it, and how they did go!
'Twas Princess and Madcap, and Ringwood and Rally,
They charmed every hill and they echoed each valley.

[4] *Bold Briton.* One of the Tickels.
[5] An old whipper-in, so called by Mr. Arscott.

From Becket, through Thorn, they went on their way,
To Swannacott Wood, without break or delay;
And when they came there, how they sounded again!
" What music it is!" cried the glad Whitstone Men.

In haste came up Arscott—" Oh, where are they gone?"
" They are off to the cliffs," then said Simon the Son;
Through Wike, and through Poundstock, St. Genys, they went,
And when Reynard came there, he gave up by consent.

So when Reynard was dead, we broke up the field,
With joy in our hearts that we made him to yield;
And when he came home he toasted the health
Of a man who ne'er varied for places or wealth!

When supper was ended we spent all the night
In gay flowing bumpers and social delight;
With mirth and good humour did cheerfully sing,
A health to John Arscott! and God save the King!

1852.

[First published in *Willis's Current Notes*, December, 1853, pp. 97-8. It is now printed as it stands in Mr. Hawker's MS. For more concerning "Arscott of Tetcott" and "Black John," the reader is referred to *Footprints of Former Men in Far Cornwall*, where he will find a most amusing chapter devoted to them.—ED.]

THE LEGEND OF SAINT CECILY.

"Brought an Angel down."

UPROSE the morning with a ruddy glow!
    Uprose her gentle forehead, wreathed with day!
The mountain-top—the wood—the river's flow,
    Gleamed softly—and aloud the matin-lay
Of singing birds, their leafy bowers below,
    Swelled into song to greet the Orient ray;
While yet the sun, full-quivered, paused on high,
To launch his arrowy beams along the sky.

Then, at the casement of his chosen bride,
    A young man listened to a sweeter song;
Fair Cecily's—of all her race the pride—
    What eye could greet a lovelier in the throng?
To win her vows how many a knight had sighed,
    With mortal love her virgin life to wrong:
But what was earth with all its golden glare?
Her eyes were heavenward, and her soul was there.

The maiden chants, her Saviour's grace to sing;
    Her harp is mingled with that thrilling sound;
The music trembles on the quivering string,
    Like some sweet sorcery of enchanted ground.
Well might an Angel-hand the magic bring,
    That first in sainted Cecily was found—
The spell that bade the awful organ roll
The storm of music o'er the shuddering soul.

The youth drew near with glad and blushing brow,
   "It is the day," he said, "the morning beams!
Friends wait with anxious ears our uttered vow—
   See! on the temple-dome the sunlight gleams;
The wreath, the sacrifice are ready now;
   The multitude along the pathway streams—
Lo! the priests beckon, and the guests are loud,
And the wide gates enfold a gathering crowd."

She lifted up her voice. "What then? Shall I,
   The vassal of the Lord, become thy slave,
To live a common life beneath the sky!
   I, that my vows to Jesu-Master gave?
He, the good Shepherd, rules me with His eye,
   My God to follow, and thy wrath to brave!
Would that thou durst at yon true altar stand,
Where I am safe, amid the Angel-band."

Mute with deep sorrow, still he stood, and stern;
   Away! away! a sad and last adieu!
And yet, fond hope, his lingering feet return,
   Once more the sorrow of her eye to view:
He smiled, to hide the love that yet would yearn;
   "Hast thou," he said, "an angel tried and true?
Show me thy friend! let me but see him shine!
My heart shall bend to thee! thy God be mine."

"It shall be done!" the unshrinking maiden said,
   "The Lord will yield His trusting handmaid grace;"
The bridegroom went, with slow and mournful tread,
   Once more, at evening-tide, that path to trace.

He came! he saw! O vision fair and dread!
  The maiden at the altar bowed her face;
Her starry eyes were rapt in trusting prayer,
And o'er that brow an Angel stood, on air!

Death-tokens held that spirit in his hand!
  He laid a rose upon the young man's breast.
The maiden took a lily of the land—
  Those flowers, the symbols of a martyr's rest;
Thereby the twain could meekly understand
  That life would fleetly fade and death was best.
Both fell for God! and now in every tongue
Valerien lives, and Cecily is sung.

[First published in *The Lamp*, July 3, 1858. Reprinted, with the following legend, in *Cornish Ballads*.

THE LEGEND OF SAINT THEKLA.

The First Lily in the Garden of God.

SWEET is the shrinking image of the rose
    When her first blush is o'er the mossy ground:
Her brow is bent where many a blossom grows:
    She gazes on the flowers that shine around
Till with the breath of spring her spirit glows,
    And her young branch with lifted leaves is crowned
Then must her eyes be raised from that low sod,
She bares her breast to heaven and yields her hues to
        God.

Such was the maiden of my lay. In youth
  She hid her beauty in her father's halls:
He who had wooed her with the words of truth,
  Like moonlight on the snow, his image falls
Upon her vestal spirit :—yet in sooth
  No nobler knight in the high festivals
Of his own city sought a chosen bride:
He was her father's choice, her own dear mother's pride.

Then came Saint Paul the Apostle to those streets;
  Castled Iconium was the city's name:
He came—he taught—how Thekla's bosom beats:
  How his deep language shook her silent frame!
She stood—she listened—till her soul entreats
  The birth of baptism, and its hallowing name:
The words are uttered and the waters poured,
She breathes the virgin-troth that binds her to the Lord.

Unheard the bridegroom's voice, and vain his vow,
  In the sweet bondage of the faith to share;
Her high resolves a father may not bow,
  She will not soften at a mother's prayer;
Till, with revolted heart and quivering brow,
  The youth will wreak on her his mad despair;
On, to the judgment-seat, with reckless breath,
And there reveals her creed whose doom is angry death.

See! in her city-gate the maiden stands!
  The threat—the promise—all are urged in vain;

She folds upon her breast her faithful hands—
   That calmness in her eye is half-disdain!
She hears the mandate to the soldier-bands,
   "To the wild beasts!" nor will she then complain,
Though Gentile hearts were moved, and many an eye
Wept to behold her led, all innocent, to die!

She stood, with gentle and uplifted look,
   When they had loosed the lions on their prey:
But lo! the fierce and famished creatures shook,
   And crouching at her feet in fondness lay;
There will they rest, though none beside may brook
   Their furious fangs nor soothe their angry way:
"The fire! the flame!" Hark, what fierce accents rise!
"Yea! scorch her to the gods! there shall be sacrifice."

A miracle again! another sign!
   The unseen Angel of the Lord was there;
They saw the flames, subdued, around her shine,
   And mingle harmless with her waving hair:
And lo! a starry Cross, as on a shrine,
   Beamed on the forehead of that maiden fair,
The first bright daughter of the Church, whose fame
Hath won in many a land the martyr's sainted name.

[Published in *The Lamp*, July 17, 1858.]

MIRIAM: STAR OF THE SEA.

I AM the Sea, that, treacherous, swells for ever,
    And ebbs and flows with one unceasing stream!
Thou art the Star, whose radiance faileth never,
    Calm o'er the billows waves its faithful beam!

I am the Sea! whose restless surges tremble,
    Moved to and fro by every sigh of night;
Thou art the Star! thy shining eyes resemble
    The orb that 'mid the storms is hushed and bright!

My Morning Star! the shades of sorrow banish;
    Kindle me hope and bravery in my soul;
Let care's dark shadows from my spirit vanish,
    As mountain-clouds before the Orient roll!

My Star of Eve! let thy sweet presence often
    Shed on this heart of mine its soothing ray!
Yea, in the War of Death thy light shall soften
    The last stern foeman, and his battle-day!

Fear's idle dream, and Hope's all-shadowy pleasure—
    Sorrow and joy, that vain and idle be—
The deep hath swallowed up the golden treasure:
    Soothe thou the tempest, and subdue the sea!

Wave after wave rolls on in ceaseless billow;
    Age cannot tame th' unconquerable tide!
Yon visible surge is but the stately pillow
    Where the wild storms of ancient waters died!

Thou Star of Peace! glory and gladness blending,
   Here as we lowly kneel, look love on high;
Hail, blessèd orb! alive with light, descending,
   A lamp to lead us to our native sky!

[Published in *The Lamp*, August 7, 1858.]

THE BIER OF MARY, MOTHER OF GOD.

A LEGEND.

SOFT eve comes down upon her couch of cloud,
   The shadows gather round the dreams of night;
With woeful psalms Jerusalem is loud,
   And far and near the funeral torch is bright;
Even the dull feet of age have sought the crowd,
   To watch with anxious eyes a shuddering sight;
From yonder home a silent corpse they bear,
The dead, the beautiful, the cold, the fair!

They wail for one—holiest of all her race—
   For Mary, maiden Mother of the Lord;
The name that, graven in stars, the angels trace,
   Hallowed in Heaven, and on earth adored,
What eyes shall yet be lifted to that face!
   What voices at those feet one day be poured,
When Angel-harps the Queen of Heaven declare,
And the Son listens to his Mother's prayer!

Holy, and full of Heaven her race was run,
   Her soul made haste to meet her glorious Child ;
He, when the rest had fled, besought Saint John
   To choose for his own Mother Mary mild.
Yea, His last thought was hers, when the sad sun
   Grew dark, and earthquake, fierce and wild,
Rent shuddering Calvary, and air and sky
Shook to behold the Hosts of Heaven pass by.

They glide, like shadows, silent, dim, and pale,
   Kinsfolk and strangers throng the peopled street ;
Forth at the gate the minstrel leads the wail,
   And on the mourners move with lingering feet.
Hark ! what stern voices rise ! what sounds prevail !
   A cry, as when in battle, foemen meet ;
A circumciséd Jew ! O, deed of fear,
Foamed at the dead, and smote that Awful Bier ;

But lo ! a doom ! That fierce and lifted hand
   Fell, quivering fell, severed by touch unseen,
The multitude are mute ; they understand
   That girded Angels guard the sacred scene ;
But he, the wretch, clings to that funeral band,
   With jabbering cry, and rent and tortured mien ;
Low, at the rested bier he bends, and there
Shrieks to the Merciful a loud and penitent prayer.

God heard him. God beheld the gushing tear ;
   His heart was visible to the Eyes divine ;
The deep thoughts of his quivering soul were clear
   As jewels, 'mid the earthquake, in the mine ;

He lifts his arms once more above the bier,
  And clothed with flesh from Heaven, new fingers shine;
He knelt a Hebrew foe in deed and word,
He rose a Christian man, disciple of the Lord.

In sad Gethsemane, in a chosen grave,
  For a set time they laid their blessèd dead;
There lilies love to bloom and boughs to wave,
  And many a murmured orison was said.
There burned the nightly star, whose radiance gave
  Sign of the sepulchre to Christian tread;
There, too, the chanted psalm was heard at eve,
When harps of heaven were touched and Angels came to grieve.

[This Legend was published in *The Lamp* for August 14, 1858.]

LINES OF DEDICATION TO H.R.H. THE PRINCE OF WALES,

IN BLIGHT'S "ANCIENT CROSSES AND OTHER ANTIQUITIES IN EAST AND SOUTH CORNWALL."

HAIL! Prince and Duke! no happier name
  Than thine amid our hills can stand,
To blend Old England's antique fame
  With castled Cornwall's rocky land!
Thy Plume, our banner of the West,
The blind Bohemia's faithful crest!

TO H.R.H. THE PRINCE OF WALES.

Void was the land in days of yore,
    Of warrior-deed and minstrel-song:
The unknown rivers sought the shore,
    The nameless billows rolled along :—
Till Arthur, and the Table-round,
Made stern Tintadgel storied ground ;

Then shone the days of spear and shield :
    When Cornwall's Duke was England's pride !
He won, on Creci's distant field,
    The spurs that gleamed on Tamar-side :
The wreath at dark Poictiers he wore
Was heather from our Cornish shore !

Spell of the past! thy knightly name
    May well the thrilling days recall
When heroes fought their fields of fame
    And minstrels chanted in the hall
Till the last trophy stood, alone,
Yon Syrian Cross in Cornish stone !

But lo ! the hills with grass are bright ;
    The valleys flow with rippling corn :
Tall cliffs that guard the couch of night,
    Greet with calm smile the lip of morn :
And, revelling in his summer caves,
Old Ocean laughs with all his waves ![1]

[1] πόντιων τε κυμάτων,
ἀνήριθμον γέλασμα.

Is not all the imagery of this striking passage drawn from the ear ?

Hail! Heir of Thrones! beneath thy smile
  We bend, where once our fathers bent:
And gather, with a shadowy toil,
  Stones for a nation's monument!
Our kindling spell for Hope and Fame,
Duke of the West! thy native name!
1858.

TO ALFRED TENNYSON, LAUREATE, D.C.L.

ON HIS "IDYLLS OF THE KING."

THEY told me in their shadowy phrase,
  Caught from a tale gone by,
That Arthur, King of Cornish praise,
  Died not, and would not die!

Dreams had they, that in fairy bowers,
  Their living warrior lies;
Or wears a garland of the flowers
  That grow in Paradise!

I read the Rune with deeper ken,
  And thus the myth I trace:—
A bard should rise, mid future men,
  The mightiest of his race.

He would great Arthur's deeds rehearse,
  On grey Dundagel's shore;
And so, the King, in laurelled verse,
  Shall live, and die no more!

August, 1859.

AISHAH SCHECHINAH.

A SHAPE, like folded light, embodied air,
    Yet wreath'd with flesh and warm;
All that of heaven is feminine and fair,
    Moulded in visible form.

She stood, the Lady Schēchĭnăh of earth,
    A chancel for the sky;
Where woke, to breath and beauty, God's own birth,
    For men to see Him by.

Round her, too pure to mingle with the day,
    Light, that was life, abode;
Folded within her fibres meekly lay
    The link of boundless God.

So link'd, so blent, that when, with pulse fulfill'd,
    Moved but that infant hand,
Far, far away, His conscious Godhead thrill'd,
    And stars might understand.

Lo! where they pause, with intergathering rest,
    The Threefold and the One!
And lo! He binds them to her orient breast,
    His Manhood girded on.

The Zone, where two glad worlds for ever meet,
    Beneath that bosom ran:
Deep in that womb, the conquering Paraclete
    Smote Godhead on to man!

Sole scene among the stars, where, yearning, glide
  The Threefold and The One:
Her God upon her lap, the Virgin-Bride,
  Her Awful Child, her Son.

May, 1859.

NOTES.

Aishah, the Native Name of Woman.

This was the happy name of Eve in the days of her innocence. When she stood before Adam in her blameless beauty, he said, being inspired, "She shall be called Aishah," that is to say, man's, or man's own, because she is taken out of Aish, "man." It was afterwards, when she had shuddered into sin, that the man called the name of his wife Eve. Now the household word for the sinless Mother in the cottage at Nazareth, and on the lips of her Son, was also Aishah; it was in memory of the former phrase of Eden, a sound of mingled endearment and respect. It was not, in that native language, as it is in our own mean and meagre speech, a mere appellative of sex, "woman," but Aishah, the tender and the graphic title of the twain: the bride of the garden, man's own, all innocent: and of Mary, maiden-Mother of God. So at Cana, and on Calvary, Jesus made chosen utterance of that only name, Aishah. At the marriage, when, with her woman's zeal for the honour of the feast, the Mother made haste to her Son, and said suddenly, "They have no wine," Jesus answered, and with the long-accustomed smile, "What have *we*, Aishah?" He said in the exact letter, "What is to Me, and to thee, Aishah?" He signified, with a very usual idiom, "What have I, and what hast thou, Aishah?" He meant in the spirit of His voice and smile, "What have we *not*, Aishah? Are not all things under our feet? Mine hour, the hour that thou wottest of, is not yet come; but still"—and the well-known look of Nazareth and home revealed the rest. So she turned to the servants and said, "Whatsoever He shall say unto you, do."

Schēchīnăh.

This, the cloudy signal of the Presence, is the most majestic symbol of Our Lady throughout the oracles. The sacramental element of the Schēchīnăh, which I have named "Numyne," was called by the Rabbins, "Mater et Filia Dei," and was always a feminine noun. They say it was a stately pillar, or column of soft and fleecy cloud, which took ever and anon, as to Elias upon

Carmel, the outline of a human shape or form, "Vestigium hominis." Within its breast sojourned the glory of the Presence, as in a tent. Therefore I claim, with all reverence, the right to use the title "Aishah Schēchīnăh." The sound of this latter word is a dactyle.

[Printed, at first, privately; then as appendix C in the first edition of *The Quest*, 1864. Dr. Lee reprints it in his *Memorials*, adding that "it seems to many almost inspired!" The *Notes* were not reprinted in *Cornish Ballads*.—ED.]

THE SOUTHERN CROSS.

THREE ancient men in Bethlehem's cave,
    With awful wonder stand:
A voice had called them from their grave,
    In some far Eastern land.

They lived: they trod the former earth,
    When the old waters swelled,
The Ark, that womb of second birth,
    Their house and lineage held.

Pale Japhet bows the knee with gold,
    Bright Sem sweet incense brings,
And Cham the myrrh his fingers hold:
    Lo! the three Orient Kings.

Types of the total earth, they hailed
    The signal's starry frame;
Shuddering with second life, they quailed
    At the Child Jesu's Name.

> Then slow the Patriarchs turned and trod,
>   And this their parting sigh:
> "Our eyes have seen the living God,
>   And now—once more to die."

Feast of the Epiphany, 1859.

The Southern Cross.

It is chronicled in an old Armenian myth, that the Wise Men of the East were none other than the three sons of Noe, and that they were raised from the dead to represent, and to do homage for all mankind, in the cave of Bethlehem. Other legends are also told: one that these patriarch princes of the flood did not ever die, but were rapt away alive into Enoch's paradise, and were then recalled to begin the solemn gesture of world-wide worship to the King-born Child. Another saying holds, that when their days were full, these Arkite fathers fell asleep, and were laid at rest in a cavern of Ararat, until Messias was born, and that then an angel aroused them from the slumber of ages to bow down and to hail as the heralds of many nations the Awful Child. Be this as it may, whether the Mystic Magi were Sem, Cham, and Japhet, in their first or second existence, under their own names, or those of other men; or whether they were three long-descended and royal sages from the loins or the land of Balaam—one thing has been delivered for very record, that supernatural shape of clustering orbs, which was embodied suddenly from surrounding light, and framed to be the beacon of their westward way, *was and is* the Southern Cross. It was not a solitary signal-fire, but a miraculous constellation: a pentacle of stars whereof two shone for the Transome, and three for the Stock, and which went above and before the travellers day and night radiantly, until it came and stood over where the young Child lay. And then! what then? must these faithful orbs dissolve and die? shall the gleaming trophy fall? Nay—not so. When it had fulfilled the piety of its first-born office, it arose, and amid the vassalage of every stellar and material law, it moved onward and on, obedient to the impulse of God the Trinity, journeying evermore towards the South, until that starry image arrived in the predestined sphere of future and perpetual abode: to bend, as to this day it bends, above the Peaceful Sea, in everlasting memorial of the Child Jesus—The Southern Cross.

[First printed above the signature "Nectan" in a Plymouth newspaper, then published with *The Quest*, as an appendix, 1864. Reprinted in *Cornish Ballads* as "The Mystic Magi."—Ed.]

KING ARTHUR'S WAES-HAEL.

THE RUBRIC.

When the brown bowl is filled for yule, let the dome or upper half be set on; then let the waes-haelers kneel one by one and draw up the wine with their reeds through the two bosses at the rim. Let one breath only be drawn by each of the morice for his waes-hael. (*Waes* in this word is sounded Waze.)

WAES-HAEL for knight and dame!
  O! merry be their dole;
Drink-hael! in Jesu's name
  We fill the tawny bowl;
But cover down the curving crest,
Mould of the Orient Lady's breast.

Waes-hael! yet lift no lid:
  Drain ye the reeds for wine.
Drink-hael! the milk was hid
  That soothed that Babe divine;
Hushed, as this hollow channel flows,
He drew the balsam from the rose.

Waes-hael! thus glowed the breast
  Where a God yearned to cling;
Drink-hael! so Jesu pressed
  Life from its mystic spring;
Then hush, and bend in reverent sign,
And breathe the thrilling reeds for wine.

Waes-hael! in shadowy scene,
   Lo! Christmas children we;
Drink-hael! behold we lean
   At a far Mother's knee;
To dream, that thus her bosom smiled,
And learn the lip of Bethlehem's Child.

1860.

NOTE.

The rounded shape of the bowl for waes-hael was intended to recall the image of a mother's breast; and thus it was meant, with a touching simplicity, to blend the thought of our Christmas gladness with the earliest nurture of the child Jesus.

[Printed in *Notes and Queries*, second series, xi., 4, and signed "Ben Tamar"; serves as Appendix D. in the first edition of *The Quest*, 1864, and is reprinted in *Cornish Ballads*.—ED.]

SIR BEVILLE.—THE GATE SONG OF STOWE.

ARISE! and away! for the King and the land;
   Farewell to the couch and the pillow:
With spear in the rest, and with rein in the hand,
   Let us rush on the foe like a billow.

Call the hind from the plough, and the herd from the fold,
   Bid the wassailer cease from his revel:
And ride for old Stowe, where the banner's unrolled,
   For the cause of King Charles and Sir Beville.

Trevanion is up, and Godolphin is nigh,
   And Harris of Hayne's o'er the river;
From Lundy to Looe, "One and all!" is the cry,
   And the King and Sir Beville for ever!

Ay! by Tre, Pol, and Pen, ye may know Cornish men,
  'Mid the names and the nobles of Devon;
But if truth to the King be a signal, why then
  Ye can find out the Granville in heaven.

Ride! ride! with red spur, there is death in delay,
  'Tis a race for dear life with the devil;
If dark Cromwell prevail, and the King must give way,
  This earth is no place for Sir Beville.

So at Stamford he fought, and at Lansdown he fell,
  But vain were the visions he cherished:
For the great Cornish heart, that the King loved so well,
  In the grave of the Granville it perished.

[Written, says Mr. Godwin, at the suggestion of Miss Louisa T. Clare, 1861. It is printed in *Cornish Ballads*, 1869.—ED.]

THE COMET OF 1861.

"Terroresque de cœlo et signa magna."—S. Luc. xxi. 11.

WHENCE art thou, sudden comet of the sun?
  In what far depths of God thine orient place?
Whence hath thy world of light such radiance won
  To gleam and curve along the cone of space?[1]

[1] Space is that measured part of God's presence which is inhabited by the planets and the sun. The boundary of space is the outline of a cone, and the pathway of every planet is one of the sections of that figured form.

THE COMET OF 1861.

Why comest thou, weird wanderer of the air?
 What is thine oracle for shuddering eyes?
Wilt thou some myth of crownless kings declare,
 Scathed by thy fatal banner of the skies?

Or dost thou glide, a seething orb of doom,
 Bristling with penal fires, and thick with souls—
The severed ghosts that throng thy peopled womb,
 Whom Azrael, warder of the dead, controls?

Throne of some lost archangel, dost thou glare,
 After long battle, on that conquering height?
Vaunt of a victory that is still despair,
 A trophied horror on the arch of night?

But lo! another dream: thou starry god,
 Art thou the mystic seedsman of the sky?
To shed new worlds along thy radiant road,
 That flow in floods of billowy hair on high?

Roll on! yet not almighty: in thy wrath
 Thou bendest like a vassal to his king;
Thou darest not o'erstep thy graven path,
 Nor yet one wanton smile of brightness fling.

Slave of a Mighty Master! be thy brow
 A parable of night, in radiance poured:
Amid thy haughtiest courses, what art thou?
 A lamp to lead some pathway of the Lord!

Morwenstow, July, 1861.

[Printed, as Appendix B, in the first edition of *The Quest of the Sangraal*, 1864, and in *Cornish Ballads*, 1869.—ED.]

A CROON ON HENNACLIFF.

THUS said the rushing raven,
    Unto his hungry mate:
"Ho! gossip! for Bude Haven:
    There be corpses six or eight.
Cawk! cawk! the crew and skipper
    Are wallowing in the sea:
So there's a savoury supper
    For my old dame and me."

"Cawk! gaffer! thou art dreaming,
    The shore hath wreckers bold;
Would rend the yelling seamen,
    From the clutching billows' hold.
Cawk! cawk! they'd bound for booty
    Into the dragon's den:
And shout, for 'death or duty,'
    If the prey were drowning men."

Loud laughed the listening surges,
    At the guess our grandame gave:
You might call them Boanerges,
    From the thunder of their wave.
And mockery followed after
    The sea-bird's jeering brood:
That filled the skies with laughter,
    From Lundy Light to Bude.

A CROON ON HENNACLIFF.

"Cawk! cawk!" then said the raven,
  "I am fourscore years and ten:
Yet never in Bude Haven
  Did I croak for rescued men.—
They will save the Captain's girdle,
  And shirt, if shirt there be:
But leave their blood to curdle,
  For my old dame and me."

So said the rushing raven
  Unto his hungry mate:
"Ho! gossip! for Bude Haven:
  There be corpses six or eight.
Cawk! cawk! the crew and skipper
  Are wallowing in the sea:
O what a savoury supper
  For my old dame and me."

[First published in *All the Year Round*, and reprinted in *Cornish Ballads*.]

THE QUEST OF THE SANGRAAL.

TO
A VACANT CHAIR:
AND
AN ADDED STONE:
I CHANT
THESE SOLITARY SOUNDS.

The name Sangraal is derived from *San*, the breviate of *Sanctus*, or Saint, *Holy*, and *Graal*, the Keltic word for Vessel or Vase. All that is known of the Origin and History of this mysterious Relique will be rehearsed in the Poem itself. As in the title, so in the Knightly Names, I have preferred the Keltic to other sources of spelling and sound.—R. S. H.

HO! for the Sangraal! vanish'd Vase of Heaven!
    That held, like Christ's own heart, an hin[1] of
        blood!
Ho! for the Sangraal! . . .
                How the merry shout
Of reckless riders on their rushing steeds,
Smote the loose echo from the drowsy rock
Of grim Dundagel, thron'd along the sea!

" Unclean! unclean! ten cubits and a span,[2]
Keep from the wholesome touch of human-kind:

[1] The hin was a Hebrew measure, used for the wine of the sacrifice.

[2] The distance at which a leper was commanded to keep from every healthy person.

Stand at the gate, and beat the leper's bell,
But stretch not forth the hand for holy thing,—
Unclean, as Egypt at the ebb of Nile!"
Thus said the monk, a lean and gnarlèd man;

His couch was on the rock, by that wild stream
That floods, in cataract, Saint Nectan's Kieve:[3]
One of the choir, whose life is Orison.
They had their lodges in the wilderness,
Or built them cells beside the shadowy sea,
And there they dwelt with angels, like a dream:
So they unroll'd the volume of the Book,
And fill'd the fields of the Evangelist
With antique thoughts, that breath'd of Paradise.

Uprose they for the Quest—the bounding men
Of the siege perilous, and the granite ring—
They gathered at the rock, yon ruddy tor;[4]
The stony depth where lurked the demon-god,
Till Christ, the mighty Master, drave him forth.

There stood the knights, stately, and stern, and tall;
Tristan, and Perceval, Sir Galahad,
And he, the sad Sir Lancelot of the lay:
Ah me! that logan[5] of the rocky hills,

---

[3] Or cauldron. [See Note to "The Sisters of Glen Nectan," p. 28.]

[4] Routor, the red hill, so named from the heath which blossoms on the hill-side.

[5] Logan, or shuddering stone. A rock of augury found in all lands, a relic of the patriarchal era of belief. A child or an innocent person could move it, as Pliny records, with a stalk of asphodel; but a strong man, if guilty, could not shake it with all his force.

Pillar'd in storm, calm in the rush of war,
Shook, at the light touch of his lady's hand!

See! where they move, a battle-shouldering kind!
Massive in mould, but graceful: thorough men:
Built in the mystic measure of the Cross:—
Their lifted arms the transome: and their bulk,
The Tree, where Jesu stately stood to die—
Thence came their mastery in the field of war:—
Ha! one might drive battalions—one, alone!

See! now, they pause; for in their midst, the King,
Arthur, the Son of Uter, and the Night,
Helm'd with Pendragon, with the crested Crown,
And belted with the sheath'd Excalibur,[6]
That gnash'd his iron teeth, and yearn'd for war!
Stern was that look (high natures seldom smile)
And in those pulses beat a thousand kings.
A glance! and they were husht: a lifted hand!
And his eye ruled them like a throne of light.
Then, with a voice that rang along the moor,
Like the Archangel's trumpet for the dead,
He spake—while Tamar sounded to the sea.

"Comrades in arms! Mates of The Table Round!
Fair Sirs, my fellows in the bannered ring,
Ours is a lofty tryst! this day we meet,
Not under shield, with scarf and knightly gage,
To quench our thirst of love in ladies' eyes:
We shall not mount to-day that goodly throne,

[6] A Hebrew name, signifying "champer of the steel."

The conscious steed, with thunder in his loins,
To launch along the field the arrowy spear:
Nay, but a holier theme, a mightier Quest—
' Ho! for the Sangraal, vanish'd Vase of God!'

" Ye know that in old days, that yellow Jew,
Accursèd Herod; and the earth-wide judge,
Pilate the Roman—doomster for all lands,
Or else the Judgment had not been for all,—
Bound Jesu-Master to the world's tall tree,
Slowly to die. . . .
　　　　　Ha! Sirs, had we been there,
They durst not have assayed their felon deed,
Excalibur had cleft them to the spine!

Slowly He died, a world in every pang,
Until the hard centurion's cruel spear
Smote His high heart: and from that severed side,
Rush'd the red stream that quencht the wrath of
　　　Heaven!

" Then came Sir Joseph, hight of Arimathèe,
Bearing that awful Vase, the Sangraal!
The Vessel of the Pasch, Shere Thursday night,
The selfsame Cup, wherein the faithful Wine
Heard God, and was obedient unto Blood.
Therewith he knelt and gathered blessèd drops
From his dear Master's Side that sadly fell,
The ruddy dews from the great tree of life:
Sweet Lord! what treasures! like the priceless gems
Hid in the tawny casket of a king,—
A ransom for an army, one by one!

" That wealth he cherisht long : his very soul
Around his ark : bent as before a shrine !

" He dwelt in Orient Syria : God's own land :
The ladder foot of heaven—where shadowy shapes
In white apparel glided up and down.
His home was like a garner, full of corn,
And wine and oil; a granary of God !
Young men, that no one knew, went in and out,
With a far look in their eternal eyes !
All things were strange and rare : the Sangraal,
As though it clung to some ethereal chain,
Brought down high Heaven to earth at Arimathèe

" He lived long centuries and prophesied.
A girded pilgrim ever and anon,
Cross-staff in hand, and, folded at his side,
The mystic marvel of the feast of blood.
Once, in old time, he stood in this dear land,
Enthrall'd—for lo ! a sign ! his grounded staff
Took root, and branch'd, and bloom'd, like Aaron's rod :
Thence came the shrine, the cell ; therefore he dwelt,
The vassal of the Vase, at Avalon !

" This could not last, for evil days came on,
And evil men : the garbage of their sin
Tainted this land, and all things holy fled.
The Sangraal was not : on a summer eve,
The silence of the sky brake up in sound !
The tree of Joseph glowed with ruddy light :
A harmless fire, curved like a molten vase,

Around the bush, and from the midst, a voice:
Thus hewn by Merlin on a runic stone :—
𝔎𝔦𝔯𝔦𝔬𝔱𝔥 : 𝔢𝔩 : 𝔃𝔞𝔫𝔫𝔞𝔥 : 𝔞𝔲𝔩𝔬𝔥𝔢𝔢 : 𝔭𝔢𝔡𝔞𝔥 :

" Then said the shuddering seer—he heard and knew
The unutterable words that glide in Heaven,
Without a breath or tongue, from soul to soul—

" ' The land is lonely now : Anathema !
The link that bound it to the silent grasp
Of thrilling worlds is gathered up and gone :
The glory is departed ; and the disk
So full of radiance from the touch of God !
This orb is darkened to the distant watch
Of Saturn and his reapers, when they pause,
Amid their sheaves, to count the nightly stars.

" ' All gone ! but not for ever : on a day
There shall arise a king from Keltic loins,
Of mystic birth and name, tender and true ;
His vassals shall be noble, to a man :
Knights strong in battle till the war is won :
Then while the land is husht on Tamar side,
So that the warder upon Carradon
Shall hear at once the river and the sea—
That king shall call a Quest : a kindling cry :
' Ho ! for the Sangraal ! vanish'd Vase of God ! '

" ' Yea ! and it shall be won ! A chosen knight,
The ninth from Joseph in the line of blood,
Clean as a maid from guile and fleshly sin—

He with the shield of Sarras;[7] and the lance,
Ruddy and moisten'd with a freshening stain,
As from a sever'd wound of yesterday—
He shall achieve the Graal: he alone!'"

" Thus wrote Bard Merlin on the Runic hide
Of a slain deer: rolled in an aumry chest.

" And now, fair Sirs, your voices: who will gird
His belt for travel in the perilous ways?
This thing must be fulfilled:—in vain our land
Of noble name, high deed, and famous men;
Vain the proud homage of our thrall, the sea,
If we be shorn of God. Ah! loathsome shame!
To hurl in battle for the pride of arms:
To ride in native tournay, foreign war:
To count the stars; to ponder pictured runes,
And grasp great knowledge, as the demons do,
If we be shorn of God:—we must assay
The myth and meaning of this marvellous bowl:
It shall be sought and found:—"
       Thus said the King.

Then rose a storm of voices; like the sea,
When Ocean, bounding, shouts with all his waves.
High-hearted men! the purpose and the theme,
Smote the fine chord that thrills the warrior's soul

---

[7] The city of "Sarras in the spiritual place" is the scene of many a legend of mediæval times. In all likelihood it was identical with Charras or Charran of Holy Writ. There was treasured up the shield, the sure shelter of the Knight of the Quest. The lance which pierced our blessed Saviour's side was also there preserved.

With touch and impulse for a deed of fame.

Then spake Sir Gauvain, counsellor of the King,
A man of Pentecost for words that burn :—

"Sirs! we are soldiers of the rock and ring:
Our Table Round is earth's most honoured stone;
Thereon two worlds of life and glory blend,
The boss upon the shield of many a land,
The midway link with light beyond the stars!
This is our fount of fame! Let us arise,
And cleave the earth like rivers; like the streams
That win from Paradise their immortal name:
To the four winds of God, casting the lot.
So shall we share the regions, and unfold
The shrouded mystery of those fields of air.

"Eastward! the source and spring of life and light!
Thence came, and thither went, the rush of worlds,
When the great cone of space[8] was sown with stars.
There rolled the gateway of the double dawn,
When the mere God shone down, a breathing man.
There, up from Bethany, the Syrian Twelve
Watched their dear Master darken into day.

---

[8] Space is a created thing, material and defined. As time is *mensura motus*, so is space *mensura loci*; and it signifies that part of God's presence which is measured out to enfold the planetary universe. The tracery of its outline is a cone. Every path of a planet is a curve of that conic figure: and as motion is the life of matter, the whirl of space in its allotted courses is the cause of that visible movement of the sun and the solar system towards the star Alcyone as the fixed centre in the cone of space. [See *The Comet of* 1861," p. 167 *supra*.]

Thence, too, will gleam the Cross, the arisen wood:[9]
Ah, shuddering sign, one day, of terrible doom!
Therefore the Orient is the home of God.

"The West! a Galilee: the shore of men;
The symbol and the scene of populous life:
Full Japhet journeyed thither, Noe's son,
The prophecy of increase in his loins.
Westward[10] Lord Jesu looked His latest love,
His yearning Cross along the peopled sea,
The innumerable nations in His soul.
Thus came that type and token of our kind,
The realm and region of the set of sun,
The wide, wide West; the imaged zone of man.

"The North! the lair of demons, where they coil,
And bound, and glide, and travel to and fro:
Their gulph, the underworld, this hollow orb,
Where vaulted columns curve beneath the hills,
And shoulder us on their arches: there they throng;
The portal of their pit, the polar gate,
Their fiery dungeon mocked with northern snow:
There, doom and demon haunt a native land,
Where dreamy thunder mutters in the cloud,
Storm broods, and battle breathes, and baleful fires
Shed a fierce horror o'er the shuddering North.

[9] The "Sign of the Son of Man," the signal of the last day, was understood, in the early ages, to denote the actual Cross of Calvary; which was to be miraculously recalled into existence, and, angel-borne, to announce the advent of the Lord in the sky.

[10] Our Lord was crucified with His back towards the east: His face therefore was turned towards the west, which is always, in sacred symbolism, the region of the people.

"But thou! O South Wind, breathe thy fragrant sigh!
We follow on thy perfume, breath of heaven!
Myriads, in girded albs, for ever young,
Their stately semblance of embodied air,
Troop round the footstool of the Southern Cross,
That pentacle of stars[11]: the very sign
That led the Wise Men towards the Awful Child,
Then came and stood to rule the peaceful sea.
So, too, Lord Jesu from His mighty tomb[12]
Cast the dear shadow of his red right hand,
To soothe the happy South—the angels' home.

"Then let us search the regions, one by one,
And pluck this Sangraal from its cloudy cave."

So Merlin brought the arrows: graven lots,
Shrouded from sight within a quiver'd sheath,
For choice and guidance in the perilous path,
That so the travellers might divide the lands.
They met at Lauds, in good Saint Nectan's cell,
For fast, and vigil, and their knightly vow:
Then knelt, and prayed, and all received their God.

"Now for the silvery arrows! Grasp and hold!"

Sir Lancelot drew the North: that fell domain,
Where fleshly man must brook the airy fiend—

---

[11] [See "The Southern Cross," p. 164 *supra*.]

[12] Our Lord was laid in His sepulchre with His head towards the west: His right hand therefore gave symbolic greeting to the region of the south: as His left hand reproached and gave a fatal aspect to the north.

His battle-foe, the demon—ghastly War!
Ho! stout Saint Michael shield them, knight and knave!

The South fell softly to Sir Perceval's hand:
Some shadowy angel breathed a silent sign,
That so that blameless man, that courteous knight,
Might mount and mingle with the happy host
Of God's white army in their native land.
Yea! they shall woo and soothe him, like the dove.

But hark! the greeting—" Tristan for the West!"
Among the multitudes, his watchful way,
The billowy hordes beside the seething sea;
But will the glory gleam in loathsome lands?
Will the lost pearl shine out among the swine?
Woe, father Adam, to thy loins and thee!

Sir Galahad holds the Orient arrow's name:
His chosen hand unbars the gate of day;
There glows that heart, fill'd with his mother's blood,
That rules in every pulse, the world of man;
Link of the awful Three, with many a star.
O! blessèd East! 'mid visions such as thine,
'Twere well to grasp the Sangraal, and die.

Now feast and festival in Arthur's hall:
Hark! stern Dundagel softens into song!
They meet for solemn severance, knight and king,
Where gate and bulwark darken o'er the sea.
Strong men for meat, and warriors at the wine,
They wreak the wrath of hunger on the beeves,

They rend rich morsels from the savoury deer,
And quench the flagon like Brun-guillie [13] dew!
Hear! how the minstrels prophesy in sound,
Shout the King's Waes-hael,[14] and Drink-hael the Queen!
Then said Sir Kay, he of the arrowy tongue,
"Joseph and Pharaoh! how they build their bones!
Happier the boar were quick than dead to-day."

The Queen! the Queen! how haughty on the dais!
The sunset tangled in her golden hair:
A dove amid the eagles—Gwennivar!
Aishah![15] what might is in that glorious eye!

See their tamed lion [16] from Brocelian's glade,
Couched on the granite like a captive king!
A word—a gesture—or a mute caress—
How fiercely fond he droops his billowy mane,
And wooes, with tawny lip, his lady's hand!

The dawn is deep; the mountains yearn for day;
The hooting cairn [17] is husht—that fiendish noise,

---

[13] The golden-hill, from *brun*, "a hill," and *guillie*, "golden:" so called from the yellow gorse with which it is clothed. (It is called "Brown Willy" in these latter days.—ED.)

[14] [See Notes to "King Arthur's Waes-hael," p. 165.]

[15] [See Notes to "Aishah Schechinah," p. 162.]

[16] This appropriate fondling of the knights of Dundagel moves Villemarque to write, "qui me plaise et me charme quand je le trouve couché aux pieds d'Ivan, le mufle allongé sur ses deux pattes croisées, les yeux à demi-ouvert et revant."

[17] See Borlase, bk. iii., ch. iii. for "Karn-idzek:" touched by the moon at some weird hour of the night, it hooted with oracular sound.

Yelled from the utterance of the rending rock,
When the fierce dog of Cain barks from the moon.[18]

The bird of judgment chants the doom of night,
The billows laugh a welcome to the day,
And Camlan ripples, seaward, with a smile.

Down with the eastern bridge! the warriors ride,
And thou, Sir Herald, blazon as they pass!
Foremost sad Lancelot, throned upon his steed,
His yellow banner, northward, lapping light:
The crest, a lily, with a broken stem,
The legend, *Stately once and ever fair*;
It hath a meaning, seek it not, O King!

A quaint embroidery Sir Perceval wore;
A turbaned Syrian, underneath a palm,
Wrestled for mastery with a stately foe,
Robed in a Levite's raiment, white as wool:
His touch o'erwhelmed the Hebrew, and his word,
Whoso is strong with God shall conquer man,
Coil'd in rich tracery round the knightly shield.
Did Ysolt's delicate fingers weave the web,
That gleamed in silken radiance o'er her lord?
A molten rainbow, bent, that arch in heaven,
Which leads straightway to Paradise and God;
Beneath, came up a gloved and sigilled hand,
Amid this cunning needlework of words,
When toil and tears have worn the westering day,
Behold the smile of fame! so brief: so bright.

---

[18] Cain and his dog: Dante's version of the man in the moon was a thought of the old simplicity of primeval days.

A vast archangel floods Sir Galahad's shield:
Mid-breast, and lifted high, an Orient cruse,
Full filled, and running o'er with Numynous [19] light,
As though it held and shed the visible God;
Then shone this utterance as in graven fire,
I thirst! O Jesu! let me drink and die!

So forth they fare, King Arthur and his men,
Like stout quaternions of the Maccabee:
They halt, and form at craggy Carradon;
Fit scene for haughty hope and stern farewell.
Lo! the rude altar, and the rough-hewn rock,
The grim and ghastly semblance of the fiend,
His haunt and coil within that pillar'd home.
Hark! the wild echo! Did the demon breathe
That yell of vengeance from the conscious stone?

There the brown barrow curves its sullen breast,
Above the bones of some dead Gentile's soul:
All husht—and calm—and cold—until anon
Gleams the old dawn—the well-remembered day—
Then may you hear, beneath that hollow cairn,
The clash of arms: the muffled shout of war;
Blent with the rustle of the kindling dead!

They stand—and hush their hearts to hear the King.

---

[19] When the cone of space had been traced out and defined, the next act of creation was to replenish it with that first and supernatural element which I have named 'Numyne.' The forefathers called it the spiritual or ethereal element, *cœlum*; from Genesis i. 2. Within its texture the other and grosser elements of light and air ebb and flow, cling and glide. Therein dwell the forces, and thereof Angels and all spiritual things receive their substance and form.

Then said he, like a prince of Tamar-land—
Around his soul, Dundagel and the sea—

" Ha! Sirs—ye seek a noble crest to-day,
To win and wear the starry Sangraal,
The link that binds to God a lonely land.
Would that my arm went with you, like my heart!
But the true shepherd must not shun the fold:
For in this flock are crouching grievous wolves,
And chief among them all, my own false kin.
Therefore I tarry by the cruel sea,
To hear at eve the treacherous mermaid's song,
And watch the wallowing monsters of the wave,—
'Mid all things fierce, and wild, and strange, alone!

" Ay! all beside can win companionship:
The churl may clip his mate beneath the thatch,
While his brown urchins nestle at his knees:
The soldier give and grasp a mutual palm,
Knit to his flesh in sinewy bonds of war:
The knight may seek at eve his castle-gate,
Mount the old stair, and lift the accustom'd latch,
To find, for throbbing brow and weary limb,
That paradise of pillows, one true breast:
But he, the lofty ruler of the land,
Like yonder Tor, first greeted by the dawn,
And wooed the latest by the lingering day,
With happy homes and hearths beneath his breast,
Must soar and gleam in solitary snow.
The lonely one is, evermore, the King.
So now farewell, my lieges, fare ye well,

And God's sweet Mother be your benison!
Since by grey Merlin's gloss, this wondrous cup
Is, like the golden vase in Aaron's ark,
A fount of manha for a yearning world,
As full as it can hold of God and heaven,
Search the four winds until the balsam breathe,
Then grasp, and fold it in your very soul!

" I have no son, no daughter of my loins,
To breathe, 'mid future men, their father's name:
My blood will perish when these veins are dry;
Yet am I fain some deeds of mine should live—
I would not be forgotten in this land:
I yearn that men I know not, men unborn,
Should find, amid these fields, King Arthur's fame!
Here let them say, by proud Dundagel's walls—
' They brought the Sangraal back by his command,
They touched these rugged rocks with hues of God:'
So shall my name have worship, and my land.

" Ah! native Cornwall! throned upon the hills,
Thy moorland pathways worn by Angel feet,
Thy streams that march in music to the sea
'Mid Ocean's merry noise, his billowy laugh!
Ah me! a gloom falls heavy on my soul—
The birds that sung to me in youth are dead;
I think, in dreamy vigils of the night,
It may be God is angry with my land,
Too much athirst for fame, too fond of blood;
And all for earth, for shadows, and the dream
To glean an echo from the winds of song!

" But now, let hearts be high ! the Archangel held
A tournay with the fiend on Abarim,
And good Saint Michael won his dragon-crest !

" Be this our cry ! the battle is for God !
If bevies of foul fiends withstand your path,
Nay ! if strong angels hold the watch and ward,
Plunge in their midst, and shout, ' A Sangraal ! ' "

He ceased ; the warriors bent a knightly knee,
And touched, with kiss and sign, Excalibur ;
Then turned, and mounted for their perilous way !

That night Dundagel shuddered into storm—
The deep foundations shook beneath the sea :
Yet there they stood, beneath the murky moon,
Above the bastion, Merlin and the King.
Thrice waved the sage his staff, and thrice they saw
A peopled vision throng the rocky moor.

First fell a gloom, thick as a thousand nights,
A pall that hid whole armies ; and beneath
Stormed the wild tide of war ; until on high
Gleamed red the dragon, and the Keltic glaive
Smote the loose battle of the roving Dane !
Then yelled a fiercer fight : for brother blood
Rushed mingling, and twin dragons fought the field !
The grisly shadows of his faithful knights
Perplext their lord : and in their midst, behold !
His own stern semblance waved a phantom brand,
Drooped, and went down the war. Then cried the
    King,

"Ho! Arthur to the rescue!" and half drew
Excalibur; but sank, and fell entranced.

A touch aroused the monarch: and there stood
He, of the billowy beard and awful eye,
The ashes of whole ages on his brow—
Merlin the bard, son of a demon-sire!
High, like Ben Amram at the thirsty rock,
He raised his prophet staff: that runic rod,
The stem of Igdrasil[20]—the crutch of Raun—
And wrote strange words along the conscious air.

Forth gleamed the east, and yet it was not day!
A white and glowing horse outrode the dawn;
A youthful rider ruled the bounding rein,
And he, in semblance of Sir Galahad shone:
A vase he held on high; one molten gem,
Like massive ruby or the chrysolite:
Thence gushed the light in flakes; and flowing, fell
As though the pavement of the sky brake up,
And stars were shed to sojourn on the hills,
From grey Morwenna's stone [21] to Michael's tor,
Until the rocky land was like a heaven.

Then saw they that the mighty Quest was won!
The Sangraal swoon'd along the golden air:
The sea breathed balsam, like Gennesaret:
The streams were touched with supernatural light:

[20] Igdrasil, the mystic tree, the ash of the Keltic ritual. The Raun or Rowan is also the ash of the mountain, another magic wood of the northern nations.

[21] [See "The Saintly Names," p. 50.]

And fonts of Saxon rock, stood, full of God!
Altars arose, each like a kingly throne,
Where the royal chalice, with its lineal blood,
The Glory of the Presence, ruled and reigned.
This lasted long: until the white horse fled,
The fierce fangs of the libbard in his loins:
Whole ages glided in that blink of time,
While Merlin and the King, looked, wondering, on.

But see! once more the wizard-wand arise,
To cleave the air with signals, and a scene.

Troops of the demon-north, in yellow garb,
The sickly hue of vile Iscariot's hair,
Mingle with men, in unseen multitudes!
Unscared, they throng the valley and the hill;
The shrines were darkened and the chalice void:
That which held God was gone: Maran-atha!
The awful shadows of the Sangraal, fled!
Yet giant-men arose, that seemed as gods,
Such might they gathered from the swarthy kind:
The myths were rendered up: and one by one,
The Fire—the Light—the Air—were tamed and bound
Like votive vassals at their chariot-wheel.
Then learnt they War: yet not that noble wrath,
That brings the generous champion face to face
With equal shield, and with a measured brand,
To peril life for life, and do or die;
But the false valour of the lurking fiend
To hurl a distant death from some deep den:
To wing with flame the metal of the mine:
And, so they rend God's image, reck not who!

"Ah! haughty England! lady of the wave!"
Thus said pale Merlin to the listening King,
"What is thy glory in the world of stars?
To scorch and slay: to win demoniac fame,
In arts and arms; and then to flash and die!
Thou art the diamond of the demon-crown,
Smitten by Michael upon Abarim,
That fell; and glared, an island of the sea.
Ah! native England! wake thine ancient cry;
Ho! for the Sangraal! vanish'd Vase of Heaven,
That held, like Christ's own heart, an hin of blood!"

He ceased; and all around was dreamy night:
There stood Dundagel, throned: and the great sea
Lay, a strong vassal at his master's gate,
And, like a drunken giant, sobb'd in sleep!

["The Quest of the Sangraal" was written during the days of loneliness which followed Mrs. Hawker's death in February, 1863. Everyone must regret that the succeeding chants which were to have completed the plan of the poem were never composed.—ED.]

TO EVA VALENTINE,

ON HER SIXTH BIRTHDAY, MAY 16, 1864.

QUEEN of the months! thy starry bloom
    Floods with glad hues our Cornish combe;
    Thy birds are loud with heaven's own mirth—
Hast thou no song for Eva's birth?

TO EVA VALENTINE.

No tempest woke, no winds were wild,
To greet thy dawn, my gentle child;
But first in summer's loveliest bowers
Thy voice was heard amid the flowers.

So was thy name, the garden bride,
Thrilled at its sound with joy and pride:
Her Eden held one fatal tree:
Be earth all paradise to thee!

Ah! Eva! she, our mother, stood
At once in noon-day womanhood;
In her full eyes there could not shine
The simple witchery of thine.

Yet, 'mid the conscious trees, began
The war that won her vassal, man:
He saw his freedom in the skies,
And lost it for his lady's eyes.

So thou, when woman's love shall warm
The pulses of thy thrilling form,
Unfold, for one dear thrall to rest,
The paradise of Eva's breast.

1864.

[The Rev. William Valentine, Vicar of Whixley, Yorks, was the intimate friend of Mr. Hawker. He owned a house in Morwenstow parish, where he frequently resided. Here he brought Miss Kuczynski (whom Mr. Hawker subsequently married) as governess to his two daughters, to whom this and the following charming poems are addressed.—ED.]

TO MATILDA VALENTINE,

ON HER BIRTHDAY, JULY 17TH, 1864.

MAID of the North! a distant sky
    Kindled with light thy large dark eye;
And now within its glances rest
The soft beams of our glowing West.

Welcome that sun! its joyous ray
Smiles on Matilda's native day;
And, lo! to soothe her path are given
The happiest hues of earth and heaven.

Hail! omen of that dawning time
When Maud shall hear her marriage-chime,
And light and music, blended, greet
The pausing matron's homeward feet.

Such and so cloudless be the days
Whereon thy noon of life shall gaze;
So may a cloudless sunset shine,
    Maid of the North, for thee and thine.

1864.

"BLUE EYES MELT; DARK EYES BURN."

THE eyes that melt, the eyes that burn,
    The lips that make a lover yearn,
These flashed on my bewildered sight,
Like meteors of the northern night.

Then said I, in my wild amaze,
" What stars be they that greet my gaze?
Where shall my shivering rudder turn?—
To eyes that melt, or eyes that burn?

" Ah! safer far the darkling sea
Than where such perilous signals be;
To rock, and storm, and whirlwind turn
From eyes that melt, and eyes that burn."

[From *All the Year Round*, 1864.]

WRITTEN IN MY LADY'S DANTE.

WHAT binds me to the page? my lonely cell
    Is dim and cold: 'tis midnight's weary time—
Why am I doomed, as if by some deep spell,
    With the lone bard his spectral hill to climb?

TO SOPHIE GRANVILLE THYNNE.

The music of her voice hath breathed these words ;
    Her eye hath shone this storied page along ;
Tones have been here soft as the summer birds,
    When echoes of the eve were deep with song !

Thenceforth a charm was on the Italian lay ;
    The Florentine was blended with thy name ;
His dreams have thronged my slumbers, but for aye
    Thy shining brow amid those visions came.

'Twere a proud task, from that rich voice to learn
    These antique legends of the dreamy South ;
Ah ! no ! too oft my wayward lips would turn
    To mar the music of that thrilling mouth !

1864.

TO SOPHIE GRANVILLE THYNNE,

ON HER FIFTH BIRTHDAY.

WITH all that earth hath holy, and all that heaven hath blest,
We hail thy native morning, fairy princess of the West !
For thy father's blood is thrilling in the daughter of his race,
And thy mother's eyes are drooping in thy soft and gentle face.

TO SOPHIE GRANVILLE THYNNE.

'Tis well those eyes were kindled where the sunset floods the plains,
For the western life of Granville is bounding in thy veins;
As a queen upon the dais shall thy future footsteps stand,
Thou shalt rule our Tamar side, a born lady of the land.

Like a brook alive with gladness shall thy happy girlhood flow
Where the heavens come down to rest, on the storied hills of Stowe;
And the billowy laugh of waters along thy native shore
Shall chant thy bridal morning with the sea's exulting roar.

Ay! the children yet unborn shall arise and learn to trace
The old ancestral features, how they haunt thy matron-face;
For the self-same smile shall beam upon thine own, thy chosen knight,
That wooed the proud Sir Beville home from Stamford's gory fight.

Lady Grace once more shall waken in her fair and happy prime:
God shield thee from such tears as fell at Lansdown's fatal time!

She will glide, and she will gleam again, her children at her knee,
For her innocence and loveliness were prophecies of thee.

So now, my gentle Sophie, I have sung this native song,
To pray in votive numbers for thy happy years and long;
Till thy father's ancient line shall revive beneath thy breast,
And thy mother's living eyes on thine own sweet babe shall rest.

I hear thy days resounding, as they roll in gladness on,
'Mid other bards that greet thee, when I am hushed and gone :
For loftier tones shall waken, and happier voices flow,
To teach thy children's children the glories of old Stowe.

1864.

ICHABOD.

Hush! for a star is swallowed up in night!
    A noble name hath set along the sea!
An eye that flashed with heaven no more is bright!
    The brow that ruled the islands—where is he?

ICHABOD.

He trod the earth, a man!—a stately mould,
   Cast in the goodliest metal of his kind:
The semblance of a soul in breathing gold,
   A visible image of God's glorious mind.

Well he became his throne: even from his birth
   On him the balsam of a prince was shed;
Myriads of lowlier men, the sons of earth,
   Bent with prone neck to greet his conquering tread.

He, when the sage's soul with doubt was riven,
   Smote the dull dreamers with his prophet-rod;
He called on earth and sea to chant of heaven,
   And made the stars rehearse the truth of God!

Yea! when the demons quelled the bold and brave,
   And roused the nations with their fiendish mock,
Unmoved he met the Gadarenes, and gave
   A lordly echo from the Eternal Rock!

Where reigns he now? What throne is set for him
   Amid the nine-fold armies of the sky?
Waves he the burning sword of Seraphim?
   Or dwells a calm Archangel, crowned on high?

We cannot tell. We only understand
   He bears an English heart before God's throne;
In heaven he yearns o'er this his chosen land;
   His zeal—his vows—his prayers—are yet our own!

Die Cinerum, 1865.

[These lines were written on the death of Nicholas, Cardinal Wiseman, February 14, 1865, and published in the *Weekly Register, or Catholick Standard*. Dr. F. G. Lee reprinted them in his *Memorials* of Mr. Hawker's life, 1876. pp. 54-5.—ED.]

SIR RALPH DE BLANC-MINSTER, OF BIEN-AIME.

The Vow.

Hush! 'tis a tale of the elder time,
    Caught from an old barbaric rhyme—
How the fierce Sir Ralph, of the haughty hand,
Harnessed him for our Saviour's land.

" Time trieth troth "—thus the lady said—
" And a warrior must rest in Bertha's bed.
Three years let the severing seas divide,
And strike thou for Christ and thy trusting bride."

So he buckled on the beamy blade,
That Gaspar of Spanish Leon made;
Whose hilted cross is the awful sign,
It must burn for the Lord and His tarnished shrine.

The Adieu.

" Now a long farewell! tall Stratton Tower,
    Dark Bude! thy fatal sea;
And God thee speed in hall and bower,
    My manor of Bien-aimé.

" Thou, too, farewell, my chosen bride,
    Thou Rose of Rou-tor land;
Though all on earth were false beside,
    I trust thy plighted hand.

"Dark seas may swell, and tempests lower,
   And surging billows foam :
The cresset of thy bridal bower
   Shall guide the wanderer home,

"Oh! for the Cross in Jesu's land,
   When Syrian armies flee :
One thought shall thrill my lifted hand—
   I strike for God and thee."

The Battle.

Hark! how the brattling trumpets blare!
Lo! the red banners flaunt the air!
And see! his good sword girded on,
The stern Sir Ralph to the wars is gone!

Hurrah! for the Syrian dastards flee!
Charge! charge! ye Western chivalry!
Sweet is the strife for God's renown—
The Cross is up, and the Crescent down!

The weary warrior seeks his tent,
For the good Sir Ralph is pale and spent;
Five wounds he reap'd in the field of fame—
Five, in his blessèd Master's name.

The solemn Leech looks sad and grim,
As he binds and soothes each gory limb;
And the solemn Priest must chant and pray,
Lest the soul unhouseled pass away.

SIR RALPH DE BLANC-MINSTER.

THE TREACHERY.

A sound of horsehoofs on the sand :
And lo ! a page from Cornish land.
" Tidings," he said, as he bent the knee,
" Tidings, my lord, from Bien-aimé."

" The owl shrieked thrice from the warder's tower;
The crown-rose withered in her bower;
The good grey foal, at evening fed,
Lay in the sunrise stark and dead."

" Dark omens three ! " the sick man cried ;
" Say on the woe thy looks betide."
" Master ! at bold Sir Rupert's call,
Thy Lady Bertha fled the Hall."

THE SCROLL.

" Bring me," he said, " that scribe of fame,
Symeon el Siddekah his name :
With parchment skin, and pen in hand,
I would devise my Cornish land.

" Seven goodly manors, fair and wide,
Stretch from the sea to Tamar side ;
And Bien-aimé, my hall and bower,
Nestles beneath tall Stratton Tower.

" All these I render to my God,
By seal and signet, knife and sod :
I give and grant to Church and poor,
In franc-almoign, for evermore.

"Choose ye seven men among the just,
And bid them hold my lands in trust;
On Michael's morn, and Mary's day,
To deal the dole, and watch and pray.

"Then bear me coldly o'er the deep,
'Mid my own people I would sleep:
Their hearts shall melt, their prayers will breathe,
Where he who loved them rests beneath.

"Mould me in stone as here I lie,
My face upturned to Syria's sky;
Carve ye this good sword at my side,
And write the legend, 'True and Tried.'

"Let mass be said, and requiem sung,
And that sweet chime I loved be rung;
Those sounds along the northern wall
Shall thrill me like a trumpet-call."

Thus said he—and at set of sun
The bold Crusader's race was run.—
Seek ye his ruined hall and bower?
Then stand beneath tall Stratton Tower.

The Mort-Main.

Now the Demon had watched for the warrior's soul,
'Mid the din of war where blood-streams roll;
He had waited long on the dabbled sand,
Ere the Priest had cleansed the gory hand.

Then, as he heard the stately dole
Wherewith Sir Ralph had soothed his soul,
The unclean spirit turned away
With a baffled glare of grim dismay.

But when he caught those words of trust—
That sevenfold choice among the just,
" Ho ! ho ! " cried the fiend, with a mock at Heaven,
" I have lost but one : I shall win my seven."

[First published in *Once a Week*, February 9, 1867, (Vol. III., pp. 167-8), and reprinted in *Cornish Ballads*.]

A THOUGHT.

(SUGGESTED BY GEN. XVIII., 1—3.)

A FAIR and stately scene of roof and walls,
    Touched by the ruddy sunsets of the West;
Where, meek and molten, eve's soft radiance falls
    Like golden feathers in the ringdove's nest.

Yonder the bounding sea, that couch of God !
    A wavy wilderness of sand between ;
Such pavement, in the Syrian deserts, trod
    Bright forms, in girded albs, of heavenly mien.

Such saw the patriarch in his noonday tent :
    Three severed shapes that glided in the sun,
Till lo ! they cling, and, interfused and blent,
    A lovely semblance gleams—the Three in One !

Be such the scenery of this peaceful ground[1]—
    This leafy tent amid the wilderness:
Fair skies above, the breath of Angels round,
    And God the Trinity to beam and bless!

August 30, 1866.

[1] The residence of Arthur Mills, Esq., M.P., at Bude Haven, Cornwall.

[This poem was sent to an intimate friend.]

A CORNISH FOLK SONG.

NOW, of all the birds that keep the tree,
    Which is the wittiest fowl?
Oh, the Cuckoo—the Cuckoo's the one!—for he
    Is wiser than the owl!

He dresses his wife in her Sunday's best,
    And they never have rent to pay;
For she folds her feathers in a neighbour's nest,
    And thither she goes to lay!

He winked with his eye, and he buttoned his purse,
    When the breeding time began;
For he'd put his children out to nurse
    In the house of another man!

Then his child, though born in a stranger's bed,
    Is his own true father's son;
For he gobbles the lawful children's bread,
    And he starves them one by one!

So, of all the birds that keep the tree,
   This is the wittiest fowl!
Oh, the Cuckoo—the Cuckoo's the one!—for he
   Is wiser than the owl!

[Published in *Notes and Queries*, May, 1868, Series IV., Vol. i., p. 480.]

THE SMUGGLER'S SONG.

ON, through the ground-sea, shove!
   Light on the larboard bow!
There's a nine-knot breeze above,
   And a sucking tide below.

Hush! for the beacon fails,
   The skulking gauger's by;
Down with your studding-sails,
   Let jib and fore-sail fly!

Hurrah! for the light once more!
   Point her for Shark's-nose Head;
Our friends can keep the shore;
   Or the skulking gauger's dead!

On! through the ground-sea, shove!
   Light on the larboard bow!
There's a nine-knot breeze above
   And a sucking tide below!

[From "The Gauger's Pocket," a story in *Footprints of Former Men in West Cornwall*, 1870.]

THE FATAL SHIP.[1]

DOWN the deep sea, full fourscore fathoms down,
    An iron vault hath clutched five hundred men!
They died not, like the nations, one by one:
    A thrill! a bounding pulse! a shout! and then
    Five hundred hearts stood still, at once, nor beat
        again!

That night the Angel of the Lord beheld
    A vast battalion of the gliding dead:
Souls that came up where seething surges quelled
    Their stately ship—their throne—and now the bed
    Where they shall wait, in shrouded sleep, the Morn
        of Dread!

Fast slept the sailor-boy! A silent dream
    Soften'd his brow with smiles—his mother's face
Droops over him—and her soft kisses seem
    Warm on his cheek: what severs that embrace?
    Death! strangling death!—alive—a conscious burial-
        place!

And he, the kingly mind,[2] whose skill had planned
    That lordly bastion of the world of wave?

---

[1] H.M.S. "Captain," an ironclad turret ship, lost off Cape Finisterre on the 6th of September, 1870.

[2] Captain Cowper Coles, R.N., who designed the vessel, was on board, and went down in her.

But yesterday he stood, in proud command,
  And now a thing of nought, where ocean raves
  Above his shuddering sepulchre in the weedy caves!

The monsters of the sea will glide and glare:
  Baffled Leviathan shall roar in vain:
The Sea Kings of the Isles are castled there:
  They man that silent fortress of the main:
  Yea! in the realms of death their dust shall rule and reign!

Lord Yahvah [3] of the Waters! Thou wert there!
  Thy presence shone throughout that dark abode:
Thy mighty touch assuaged the last despair:
  Their pulses paused in the calm midst of God:
  Their souls, amid surrounding Angels, went abroad!

1870.

[3] "Yahvah," the Hebrew name of God the Trinity, wrongly spelt and pronounced "Jehovah."

[Printed in *The Sun*, 1870.]

PARAPHRASE ON THE INSCRIPTION UPON THE STATUE OF SIR T. D. ACLAND, BART.

ERECTED IN HIS HONOUR DURING HIS LIFETIME, UPON THE NORTHERNHAY, AT EXETER.

The Inscription.

"Præsenti tibi maturos largimur honores."

SLAY for the Hero at the set of sun,
   But make no offering till the day is done:
Who knows what gloom may touch the warrior's name—
What gathering clouds may quench his burning fame?

But, for the Acland, let yon statue rise,
While yet he breathes, a living sacrifice:
Make the full memory of his manhood known,
And its firm Christian mould survive in stone!

   1863.

ON READING LORD DERBY'S TRANSLATION OF HOMER.

SEVEN ancient cities strove for Homer's birth:
   Let no such rivalry divide the earth:
Hark how the bard in Stanley's audience sung,
And claimed our language for his native tongue!

   1865.

THE CORNISH EMIGRANT'S SONG.

OH! the eastern winds are blowing;
   The breezes seem to say,
"We are going, we are going,
   To North Americay.

"There the merry bees are humming
   Around the poor man's hive;
Parson Kingdon is not coming
   To take away their tithe.

"There the yellow corn is growing
   Free as the king's highway;
So, we're going, we are going,
   To North Americay.

"Uncle Rab shall be churchwarden,
   And Dick shall be the squire,
And Jem, that lived at Norton,
   Shall be leader of the quire;

"And I will be the preacher,
   And preach three times a day
To every living creature
   In North Americay."

AURORA.

SUNFALL, and yet no night! fire floods the earth!
    A molten rainbow flakes the northern sky!
The Polar gates unclose! and, gleaming forth,
    Troop the wild flames that glide and glare on high,
    Tinged in their vaulted home with that deep ruddy
        dye!

Whence flash these mystic signals? what the scene
    Where the red rivers find their founts of flame?
Far, far away, where icy bulwarks lean
    Along the deep, in seas without a name:
    Where the vast porch of Hades rears its giant
        frame!

The underworld of souls! severed in twain:
    One, the fell North, perplexed and thick with gloom;
And one, the South, that calm and glad domain,
    Where asphodel and lotus lightly bloom
    'Neath God's own Starry Cross, the shield of peaceful doom.

No quest of man shall touch—no daring keel
    Cleave the dark waters to their awful bourne;
None shall the living sepulchre reveal
    Where separate souls must throng, and pause; and
        yearn
    For their far dust, the signal, and their glad return.

P

Ay! ever and anon the gates roll wide,
  When whole battalions yield their sudden breath;
And ghosts in armies gather as they glide,
  Still fierce and vengeful, from the field of death.
  Lo! lightnings lead their hosts, and meteors glare
    beneath.

[Printed as a leaflet; having been suggested by an unusually brilliant display of the Aurora Borealis on November 10, 1870. Reprinted to the number of twenty-five copies for private circulation) by Rev. W. Maskell, 1873.—ED.]

A FRAGMENT.

MARCH month is come! With rush and roar
  He hammers at the quivering door;
The forest bends beneath the rain,
The harsh hail crackles on the pane.

But, foe more fierce than March is nigh,
A wilder weapon beats the sky;
A deadlier echo cleaves the vale,
Than crackling roof or pattering hail.

The storm is loud, but not alone:
That shout was Battle's warrior-tone!
The voice that shook yon stormy sky
Was haughty England's signal-cry!

[Not printed until now. There are no indications that will serve to date these lines, which are written upon the half of a sheet of letter-paper. They perhaps refer to the outbreak of the Crimean War.—ED.]

THE CAROL OF THE PRUSS.

HURRAH! for the boom of the thundering gun!
    Hurrah for the words they say!—
" Here's a Merry Christmas to every one,
    And a Happy New Year's Day!"
Thus saith the King to the echoing ball:
" With the blessing of God we shall slay them all!"

" Up!" said the King, " load, fire, and slay!
    'Tis a kindly signal given:
However happy on earth be they,
    They'll be happier in heaven.
Tell them, as soon as their souls are free,
They'll sing like birds on a Christmas tree!

" Down with them all! If they rise again,
    They will munch our beef and bread;
War there must be with the living men,
    There'll be peace when all are dead!
This earth shall be our wide, wide home,
Our foes shall have the world to come!

" Starve! starve them all, till through the skin
    You may count each hungry bone:
Tap! tap their veins till the blood runs thin
    And their sinful flesh is gone;
While life is strong in the German sky,
What matters it who beside may die!

" No sigh so sweet as the cannon's breath,
    No music like the gun !
Here's a Merry Christmas to War and Death,
    And a Happy New Year to none ! "
Thus saith the King to the echoing ball :
" With the blessing of God we shall slay them all ! "

December 24, 1870.

[Written at the time of the Franco-Prussian War.]

IMPROMPTU LINES,

Written in a copy of *The Cornish Ballads*, given to Mary, eldest daughter of the Rev. and Hon. Thomas Edwardes, on her ninth birthday, September 15, 1873.

MARY ! thy happy name was given
    In tones of earth, to breathe of heaven.
Hallowed by Her, the sinless Child,
The Maiden Mother, undefiled.
Oh ! with her name, her nature take,
And keep thee pure, for Mary's sake.

1873.

A CANTICLE FOR CHRISTMAS, 1874.

LO ! a pure Maiden, meek and mild,
    Yearns to embrace an awful Child !
Those limbs, her tenderest touch might win :
Yet thrill they with the God within !

A CANTICLE FOR CHRISTMAS, 1874.

She gazes! and what doth she see?
A gleaming Infant on her knee!
She pauses: can she dare to press
That Glory with a fond caress?

Yet 'tis her flesh: that Form so fair!
Her very blood is bounding there!
The mother's heart the victory won:
It is her God! it is her Son!

Hers the proud gladness mothers know,
Without a thrill, without a throe;
And Mary—Mary undefiled,
Claims for her breast that awful Child!

1874.

[Printed as a leaflet for private distribution.—ED.]

THE CHRISTMAS TREE.

SHE wandered through the city,
   A lonely poor man's child;
The hardest heart would pity
   That face so sad and mild.

She heard the joy of voices,
   For they kept their Christmas-tide;
But o'er that girl rejoices
   Her God and none beside.

It had pleased the Lord to gather
    Her parents to their rest;
Her mother and her father,
    And all who loved her best.

She saw them gaily bringing
    Gifts for the Christmas-tree;
She heard sweet children singing,
    But lone and sad was she!

"Alas!" she cried, "I only
    Am shut out from their mirth;
O! why am I so lonely?
    Thou Saviour of the Earth!"

Behold! her hand she raises,
    With wonder and affright;
On a fair strange Child she gazes,
    Clothed as in robes of light!

"I was, like thee, a stranger,
    A solitary birth;
I have gone through childhood's danger,
    And sorrows of the earth."

"My name is JESUS! yonder
    Those starry branches see;
No longer, lonely, wander,
    It is thy Christmas-tree!"

Then came an angel, gladly,
    Forth from the silvery leaves;
Down where the maiden sadly,
    Among the joyful, grieves.

"Seek thou," He said, "none other,
  Thou wanderer of the wild;
Thy father and thy mother
  Is JESUS, Mary's child!"

[From a printed leaflet, for private distribution as a Christmas Carol, date uncertain; probably about 1874. Now included in the collection for the first time.—ED.]

A DOXOLOGY.

OH awful, mystic, Three-and-One—
  The Father, Holy Ghost, and Son!
Other in person and in name:
In life and nature, GOD, the same.

The Father, first—the only Son—
The Spirit, mingling Three-in-One;
All, gathered in their sole abode,
The very and eternal GOD.

There, when our day of peace began,
Throned in their midst, Behold the Man!
Jesu! the God who died, was he—
The Second of the awful Three.

Then fame and honour ever be,
In heaven, to GOD, the Trinity!
On earth, let equal praise be done,
And worship we the Three and One.

[Found amongst Mr. Hawker's MSS., but not known to have been printed before. It may, however, like many of his effusions, have been circulated amongst his parishioners on some especial occasion. —ED.]

TRANSLATIONS.

THE FISHER.

FROM THE GERMAN OF GOETHE.

THE waters rush'd—the waters rose—
    The fisher sate thereby;
He watch'd that stream in mute repose
    Beneath the silent sky.
Was it a dream? even as he gazed
    Uproll'd the waters there,
And on their foamy breast was raised
    A maiden strange and fair!

A low sweet song she sung to him:
    "Why lure the glancing brood,
The dwellers in my native stream,
    From their mute solitude?
Knew'st thou how happy there they be
    Where the deep waters swell,
Thou could'st not choose but share with me
    The blue home where we dwell.

"Glides not the quiet moon to lave
    Her brow by this calm shore?
Thou see'st her rise from out yon wave
    More lovely than before.

Gaze on these heavens of dreamy blue,
  How soft their imaged beam!
Thine own form wears a calmer hue
  In this our happy stream!"

The waters rush'd—the waters rose—
  Around his feet they swell;
How cold and dull his bosom grows
  Beneath the Naiad's spell!
A low sweet song she sang to him
  Beside the haunted shore—
His gear lies scatter'd by the brim,
  The fisher comes no more!

1826.

[This translation is placed amongst Mr. Hawker's acknowledged poems in the first series of *Records of the Western Shore*, 1832; but it was probably written in collaboration with his first wife (if not entirely by Mrs. Hawker), who published several translations from the German, the verses of which, says Mr. Baring-Gould, "were turned with grace and facility."—ED.]

TO SPRING.

FROM SCHILLER.

WELCOME, thou blooming maiden
    Thou joy of Nature's breast,
With thy wreathéd flowers laden!
  Welcome from thy rest!

TO EMMA.

Ah! ah! as dear as ever,
   As lovely as before;
We'll forget that we must sever,
   While thou art here once more.

I think, when last thy blossom
   Was bursting on the hill,
How I won the faithful bosom
   Of Her, who loves me still.

And I think of fondly twining
   Fair flowers on her brow,
Amidst her dark hair shining—
   Such as I gather now.

So welcome! blooming maiden—
   Thou joy of Nature's breast;
With thy wreathéd flowers laden,
   Welcome! from thy rest.

1826.

TO EMMA.

FROM SCHILLER.

AMID those clouds of distant grey,
   There shines at eve one lonely star,
To tell with sad and changeful ray,
What love, and joy, and beauty are.
   Though pure and beautiful and bright,
   'Tis the frail vision of the night.

And yet, should Death's long slumber steal,
And dim the radiance of thine eye,
Still would my heart thy presence feel—
To me, to me, thou could'st not die!
    But oh! thou livest in the light
    All pure, and beautiful, and bright!

And should Love fade just like that star?
Should its hue change at morn and eve?
Ah! no, its beams should shine afar,
Unchanged, on those who love and grieve,
    Still pure, and beautiful, and bright,
    Unlike that vision of the night.

1826.

THE ALPINE HUNTER.

FROM SCHILLER.

"Thou wilt not, then, our young lambs feed,
    Our graceful lambs, along the mead?
Nor where the laughing rills of spring
O'er the wild flowers their spray shall fling?"
    "Mother! my mother! let me go
    To the far hills crown'd with snow."

"Shall not thy merry horn call home
The bleating flocks that wayward roam?

Pleasant it is, in peaceful mood,
To hear their bells ring through the wood!"
   "Mother! my mother! let me go,
   Ranging the mountains, high and low."

"These flowers of thine, so fresh and fair,
Claim from thy hands their wonted care.
No rose amid those crags has smiled
Nor breathed its perfume to the wild!"
   "Let the fair flowers in beauty blow.
   Mother! my mother! let me go."

The boy went to the distant chase,
With a wild hunter's reckless pace;
He sought untired his mountain prey,
Mid many a wild and fearful way.
   Till rushed at last the light gazelle
   From the dear haunt she loved so well.

On, on! with quivering limb she sped;
On, on! he comes with bounding tread;
O'er cleft and crag her footsteps flew,
And limbs as fleet their tracks pursue.
   Vain that wild spring! thy spareless foe
   Bears the fell shaft and fatal blow.

Then might you mark the hopeless moan,
That almost spake with human tone;
The eye that sought, with glance so bland,
For soft'ning heart or sparing hand;
   But marked not where, in wrathful mood,
   The Spirit of the Mountain stood.

"Would'st thou bring Death and Sorrow here,
And human Wrath, and human Fear?
This shaft, by thy dark hand prepared,
Shall harm no more my peaceful herd."
  How will his wrath that shaft employ?—
  It quivers in the hunter-boy.

1826.

POMPEII.

A FRAGMENT FROM SCHILLER.

OLD Earth! we knew thy pleasant lap would yield
  The shining river and the stainless spring,
Pure stones and precious metals without sum;
But deemed not, from thy dark and teeming womb
Another race should come—another kind!

Sons of old Athens! Race of giant Rome!
Behold once more Pompeii—the dark city—
The unbroken roof still shades the marble hall,
And the wide portal woos the lingering guest.

The Theatre presents her opening gates:
Ye mimes! Where linger ye?
       Come forth, come forth!
Strike, Son of Atreus! strike the ready victim!
Let the Dark Sisters hover round Orestes!

On! through yon Arch of Triumph to the Forum;
Strange figures sit in yonder curule chair.
Why not advance the fasces, ye grim Lictors?
Prætor! the weary plaintiff seeks thine ear.

Alas! there is no sound; the sculptured roof,
The path just worn by human feet; the door
That human hands have opened—these are here;
And yet, there is no sound—there is *no* sound.

Enter! the pavement glows with rich mosaic,
And the wall shines with fresh and living hues
From yonder pallet. See! with loaded basket
A laughing boy bears off the bursting cluster,
Plucked by his grandsire from the weary vine.

And see! where fresh from the warm painter's hand
Speeds the wild Bacchante her reckless dance;
Or sleeps, voluptuous, underneath the elm,
Nor has that Faun, enraptured, gazed enough.

1826.

"LORD, WHITHER GOEST THOU?"

FROM THE GERMAN.

BLOOD flowed throughout the stately city,
    The cruel Cæsar's haughty home;
Men perished, and there was no pity,
    Nor rescue, in imperial Rome.

It was when Nero's wrath was sorest,
   And death and sorrow marked his way,
When, like the wild beast of the forest,
   He revelled o'er his quivering prey.

Then Christian limbs were bowed and blended,
   Prostrate where peopled pathways meet;
Coated with slime, till pain was ended
   By the slow march of trampling feet;
Or smeared around with pitch for burning,
   Their fires along the pavement spread,
Torches to light the crowds, returning
   From some fierce game where Christians bled.

Now blessèd blood that day was sweeter
   Than the red stream of lowlier gore;
So shall the veins of good Saint Peter
   Slake the fierce Gentiles' thirst once more.
His guilt—that he the blind and cripple
   Had touched until they saw and trod;
His crime—that hosts of Roman people
   Sought at his voice the Christians' God.

Then fastly came the woeful warning
   Where the meek Church had met to sigh;
The place, the doom, the fatal morning
   When Simon, Jonah's son, shall die.
So many a loving accent pleaded—
   "Baffle with Nero's wrath, and flee;
Thine arm, thy living voice, are needed
   The succour of God's Church to be."

"LORD, WHITHER GOEST THOU?"

Their secret wish his own resembled,
   Forth from the gate his footsteps fare:
Whom did he see, that thus he trembled?
   O blessèd Jesu! Thou wert there!
"Now whither goest Thou, dear Master?"
   The Apostle said, with kindling eye.
"Once more to brook the old disaster:
   Again upon My Cross to die.

"To die for those who would have perished
   Had they been left to love like thine:
The flock thou oughtest to have cherished,
   The lambs and sheep so dearly Mine."
Thus said the Lord, and forthwith vanished,
   E'en as He did in days of yore;
And he, the Apostle, turned and banished
   The fear of death for evermore.

1858.

TENDRILS.

BY REUBEN.

"Poets are a sensitive race, whose sweetness is not to be drawn forth, like that of the fragrant grass near the Ganges, by crushing and trampling upon them."

Lalla Rookh.

CHELTENHAM:
PRINTED BY S. Y. GRIFFITH, CHRONICLE OFFICE.
PUBLISHED BY HATCHARD AND SON, AND G. WHITTAKER, LONDON;
BULGIN, BRISTOL; NETTLETON AND SON, PLYMOUTH;
BETTISON, WILLIAMS, AND ROBERTS,
CHELTENHAM.
1821

TO THE

FRIENDS OF MY EARLY BOYHOOD

THE FOLLOWING PAGES

ARE AFFECTIONATELY INSCRIBED

AND DEDICATED.

PREFACE.

WHEN a first attempt is submitted to public notice and judgment, its readers may very naturally desire to know somewat concerning him who has the temerity to make it.

But the writer of the following rhymes has little in himself to excite interest, and less to afford gratification: he is content to wrap the veil of obscurity around his head until the voice of public opinion shall have passed by.

To apologize in some measure, however, for the abundant imperfections of the first effort of his pen, he would express a hope that the productions of one over whom eighteen summers have scarcely passed will carry some excuse with them; and as his motive for thrusting them on the world, he would plead that a measure of vanity is meted to us all, and his portion has been in no wise withheld.

CHARLTON, 1821.

TENDRILS.

SONNET.

THE vine puts forth her buds—and Heaven may shed
  Its gentlest dews; and they may spring and grow,
  And rains may fall, and softening nightwinds blow,
To bid them live and multiply—and spread
  To branches clustering with goodly fruit!
But yet that vine may fade, and hang in vain,
Cumbering the ground; and there may fall no rain,
  Or dew of evening round its withered root!
Go forth, my *Tendrils*, may some fostering eye,
Smile on your weakness, and ye shall not die!

THE FAIRY VISION.

"Oh! then I see Queen Mab hath been with you."
Shakespeare.

INTRODUCTION.

THERE is a popular tradition that whoever enters a Fairy-ring at night is spell-bound, and receives the visionary faculty, until the dawn of morning dispels the charm, of communing with such spirits as may choose to visit him. On the supposition that a stranger unexpectedly discovers himself in the above-mentioned situation, the following lines are written; and their abrupt commencement with the speech of the Stranger may thus be very naturally accounted for.

The liberty I have taken with the metre will, I trust, be pardoned, when it is remembered that a regular versification would but ill accord with the nature of the subject.

Stranger.

Who art thou, form of loveliness,
With light blue eye and silken tress,
Wing like the eagle's spread for flight,
Foot of wandering, and brow of light?

Spirit.

I am a daughter of the air,
And the lands of the South are given to my care,
I slept until the morning's birth,
My pillow a cloud, and my couch the earth;
But I was call'd up from my rest,
To breathe upon a warrior's breast,
Who was fleeting away on the battle-plain,
And I won him back to life again!
Then I wav'd my pinions and sought a bower,
Where, teeming with fragrance, there budded a flower.
I hovered around and sigh'd o'er its brow,
Till it burst into life, and is flourishing now.

THE FAIRY VISION.

I was sent to the bed of a dying man,
And slow in his veins the life-blood ran,—
I fanned with my wings the fever of death,
And bare away gently his parting breath.
I stole to a place where a maiden was weeping,
And long had her heart a sad vigil been keeping,
But true were her vows though cherish'd in grief,
And her tear on my wing was as dew to the leaf;
A sigh full of hope I breathed on her bosom,
And her cheek bloomed afresh like a rain-wash'd blossom!
A bark was sailing and a lover it bare
To one who was faithful, and chaste, and fair:
I filled the sail, and it swiftly rode on,
Till the place of love and hope was won.
Stranger! many deeds have I done,
With the dawn, and the noon, and the fall of the sun.
The sunset is gone, and the evening advances,
And moonbeams are throwing their loveliest glances;
And now in the dewdrops I freshen my limbs,
And fly where the air-sylphs are chanting their hymns;
I perfume my wings with the breath of the rose,
And the sigh of the violet where sweetest it grows.
Then light in my gladness I wanton away,
Where soft eyes are shining with love in their ray;
I play witn each ringlet that curls o'er her brow,
And in gentleness murmur my whispering vow,—
But the stars are come forth in their chariots of blue,
And I mount up to greet them,—
      Stranger, adieu!

Stranger.

Soft breasted Spirit! peace and love
Go with thee to thy dwelling above,
Wherever thy rose-strewn way thou wingest,
Wherever the breath of gladness thou bringest.
But, lo! a fair sister of beauty is nigh,
And her form wears the tint of an evening sky
When the sun throws off his robe of splendour,
When his smile is soft and his shining tender.
On her brow the rose and the myrtle-wreath meet,
And the pinions of a dove spread from her feet;
Her cheeks are all bloom and her eyes all brightness,
And a lyre she is sweeping with fingers of lightness.

Spirit (*sings*).

By the first rose of spring, when its fragrance is sweetest,
By the nightingale's song, when her coming is fleetest,
By the tender light of the evening beam,
By the whispering breeze and flowing stream,
By the stars that nightly shine over the sea,
Mortal! I charge thee, listen to me!
I come from a lovely and blessed place,
   Where birds never die and leaves never fall,
Where the winds steal on and leave no trace,
   And a rainbow light melts over all.
I come, and the flowers spring fresher around,
And wherever I tread it is magical ground;—
I watch where the blossoms of harmony swell,
And the soul of the minstrel I charm with a spell;

Wherever he wanders, I am hovering by,
At the first of the morn, and when evening is nigh,
To the mood of his spirit, the night is not dim,
For I brighten the stars of the heaven for him;
Though mantled in clouds, the morning is sweet,
For I strew with fair flowers the path of his feet,—
O'er the curl of the fountain, the foam of the sea,
The bloom of the field, and the leaf of the tree,
O'er the clouds that roll on with the storm in its breast,
And the mist that comes down on the mountain to rest,
O'er the raindrop of morn, and the evening tear,
My magic I breathe, and to him they are dear!
There are hearts where I dwell, and bright eyes where I shine,
There are visions I form, and fair chaplets I twine.
  In the ebb and the flood,
   From the birth to the tomb,
  From the myrtle's first bud
   To the laurel in bloom,
I watch o'er the children of Poetry's love
While their bosoms are glowing with flame from above.
But the flowers are opening to welcome the day.
Stranger mortal—away! away!

Stranger.

There's a chain that is golden entwined round my heart,
It is linked by delight—and I *may* not depart

Though sorrow befell me I would not away,
While visions so sweet, so beautiful, stay.
Another is with me—

     And who art *thou*,
With a milk-white bird on thy Angel brow,
Blooming thy cheek, though tearful thine eye,
Mingling the smile on thy lip with a sigh?

SPIRIT.

Hast thou a sorrow?—come, tell it to me,
Have I a comfort?—thine it shall be,—
I seek where the tears of the mourner are flowing,
 And breathe on his brow till its throbbing is calm;
I steal where the heart of the chastened is glowing,
 And as rain to the flower my smile is his balm.
Where the exile is wandering my pinions are nigh,
Where the pilgrim is weary, to soothe him am I.
I whisper them tales of the home of their youth,
Of the hearts that are fond, and the prayers that are truth.
I fly where the sailor-boy watches aloft,
And though storms gather round him his slumbers are soft.
Then I bear his young spirit away on my wings,
Where the thrush that he lov'd in his childhood still sings;
Where the woodbine is 'twining its wreaths on the wall,
And dear ones again on their wanderer call;—
There is one bending o'er him whose lip cannot speak,
And the tear of affection falls warm on his cheek.

There is one standing near him with words in her eye,
And he seeks the embrace which she may not deny;—
But the sea-bird sails past—and shrill is her scream,
And in tears he awakens, but blesses his dream.
The sigh of the lonely—the teardrop of pain,
Where hope is wasted, and prayers are vain,—
The lips that are pale, the cheeks that are wan,
Where joy is bitter—and comfort is gone,—
The flowers that fade where the spring-blight is flying,
The leaves that are falling, the birds that are dying,
The blasted sapling, the withering tree,
Are sacred to Pity, and cherished by me.
Peace to thee, peace!
     I have yet far to go;
There are streams on the earth and their fountain is woe:
There are hearts that are breaking, and wounds none can bind,
There are brows that are drooping, and balm I must find.

The voice of the FOURTH SPIRIT *is heard.*

Thou see'st me not, mortal, and yet I am nigh,
Where flowers spring around thee, and stars are on high.
I burst into life from the cradle of day,
And shine where the waters steal evening away;
Where the rose is unfolding I sleep on its leaves,
And smile where the lily in loneliness grieves,—
To the rock that by sea-waves of summer is kiss'd,
To the hill when the autumn hath robed it in mist,

I come in the pride of my loveliest smile,
And the breath of the south-wind plays round me the
    while.
I rest on the billow that curls from the deep,
Till its breast, like an infant, is murmur'd asleep:
By the wanderer then I am seen from afar,
My robe is a moonbeam, my crown is a star.
I glide o'er the waters with thought-speeding feet,
My paths they are lovely, my smiles they are sweet;
I fly to the earth on the pinions of spring,
With life in my bosom, with bloom in my wing,
Where nature is fairest my footsteps have been,
Where bowers are fruitful, where valleys are green;
  Stranger, there's not a lovely hue,
   Where summer flowers shine,
    There's not a charm thine eye can view,
     That is not mine,—
I was sent with the sun, from my birthplace above,
The spirit of Beauty, the chosen of Love!

    STRANGER.

Farewell to thee, angel of sweetness, farewell!
There's a charm in thy presence—thy voice is a spell.
It will live in my memory for many a year,
At the opening of spring, and when summer is near,
And when autumn is breathing her sighs to the gale,
The lip of wild Fancy shall murmur thy tale.
But there is one stealing now on my sight,
Like a mellow'd ray of heaven's own light,
Robed in the cloud of a rainless sky,
A blush on her cheek, and a smile in her eye,

A chaplet of lilies is wreath'd in her tresses,
And she plays with the wind like a hawk from her jesses.

Spirit.

I may not come near thee, thou hast tasted of sin,
My path will not be where thy footsteps have been,
I may not come down where thou breathest the air,
Lest I sully my robe with the guilt that is there.
Mortal of sorrow, thou know'st me not now,
Yet the time it hath been when I dwelt on thy brow,
When thy lips to the bosom of Innocence clung,
And her's were the accents that flowed from thy tongue.
I dwell in a valley where man never trod,
Where daisies and snowdrops are spangling the sod.
There's a stream flowing through with its silvery wave,
And sunlight the purest the sky ever gave,
There are lambs sporting onward to drink of that stream,
And turtle-doves spreading their wings to that beam
There are eyes full of love which all passionless shine,
On the babes who come hither while yet they are mine.
The sighs that are sinless float there from the earth,
And the whispering hope that is pure in its birth,
They come, and the breeze bears them gently along,
Till they melt into music, and sweet is their song!
It speaks of the vows that for ever endure,
The hearts that are changeless—the love that is pure;

They come in their sweetness, and steal through the air
To my fostering bosom, and nestle them there.—
 Stranger! Stranger! would'st thou seek
  Where my *earthly* dwelling is won?
 I bloom in childhood's rubied cheek,
  Mellowing to affection's sun;
 My home is the guileless lip of youth,
  The eye, pure as light from above,
 The smile of Beauty pledging her truth,
  The painless sigh, whose spirit is love.
They are mine—and oh! that they never would cease,
In my bower of gladness to whisper me peace,
But they fly from the bosom that nursed them in vain,
And their songs are but sorrow, their murmurs but pain.
Fare thee well! for the light of the morning is near,
For thy sins, child of darkness, I leave thee my tear.

Chorus of Fairies.

First Fairy.

 Stranger, away! the stars on high
  Are rayless and dim,
 And there is music in the sky,
  'Tis the lark's sweet hymn.

Second.

There's a flower beside thee and the dewdrops hang on,
As if they were weeping the moon that is gone;

On the brow of yon mountain there glitters a ray,
'Tis the glance of the morning, the first smile of day.

Third.

On the mist we rode down from our mansions of blue,
With a cloud for our chariot, we bid thee adieu—
The sun beam'd upon us his last look of light,
The stars shone above, and the moonbeams were bright;
But they all are departed—their beauty is o'er:
Our charms they are broken—our spells are no more.

All.

Son of earth! farewell, thine eyes have seen
    What never again they may see;
For no more in our revelry-bower of green
    Will a spell for the wanderer be.
      Uncharm'd is the sod
    Where a mortal hath trod,
      While weeps the midnight dew,
And Fairies no more
Will wander o'er
    The place where we bid thee adieu.

HOME.

A FRAGMENT.

"There's a bliss beyond all that the minstrel has told,
   When two, that are link'd in one heavenly tie,
With heart never changing and brow never cold,
   Love on through all ills, and love on till they die!"
Moore.

IN days of boyhood, when young Feeling springs
   Fresh from the heart, on Hope's unblighted wings,
When Innocence enthron'd on Beauty's brow,
Hath won the soul and taught the heart to bow;
Fair are the visions of the youthful breast,
Of bowers of happiness and homes of rest,
Of vows that change not, lips that know not guile,
And love for ever bright in woman's smile.
Lo! the proud sunbow bends its arch of light,
And earth is lovelier and heaven more bright,
The Guebre[1] kneels to breathe his whisper'd prayer,
He turns to worship—and it is not there,
Or veil'd in mist its fading hues remain,
Melt into clouds, and speak his homage vain.
So shines o'er life while yet a waveless stream

---

[1] The Guebres were a sect of ancient Persians who worshipped the sun, and the rainbow they esteemed a peculiar manifestation of his favour. "On the appearance of this 'beautiful wonder,' they prostrated themselves on the earth, toward the sun, muttering inwardly a form of adoration; after which they arose and repeated their prostrations to the rainbow while it remained visible, and according to the shortness or length of its duration, they supposed their deity to be more or less propitious."

The star of hope with silver-vested beam ;
So flow the vows from early feeling's tongue,
When her soft harp by Beauty's hand is strung,
And thus for ever fade that light, that tone,
E'er we can hail their loveliness our own.

Yet are there some, like beacons o'er the deep,
Or forms that comfort when the weary sleep,
Lamps to our path and stars to guide our way,
Truth in their light and beauty in their ray ;
Theirs that pure flame, the magic of *the mind*,
A charm to lure us, and a spell to bind !
Dear to the heart in after-days of wrath
Our infant joys, and childhood's thornless path;
For ever dear the life-bestowing breast,
The arms that held us and the lips that prest.
But dearer, lovelier yet, are those that claim
Our all of feeling in affection's name ;
Dearer to eyes that weep, and feet that roam,
Love's olive bower, an angel-guarded home.

'Tis worth an age of wandering to return
To souls that still can feel, and hearts that burn ;
We have not bent the chasten'd brow in vain,
To hear the whisper, "Thou art mine again !"
To see in eyes we love the tear-drop swell
With more of feeling than the lip could tell.
The weary pilgrim's wish—the exile's prayer,
Breathe of their home—that they may wander there,
And like the sun when summer days are past,
Sink into rest, their calmest hour their last,

Heave the death-sigh where those around will weep,
And sleep for ever where their fathers sleep.

Even in the desert will the night-bird sing,
And track the mountain with her lonely wing;
Where woods are wild the rose of spring will bloom,
Unveil her brow, and breathe her sweet perfume.
In strains as soothing, and in hues as fair,
Warbles that bird, and springs that flow'ret there
As if their birth-place were the haunt of men,
Or heaven smiled on them in the water'd glen.
And true the faith that woman's love should claim,
When chaste the whispered vow and pure the flame,
True in all climes, from Asia's burning sky,
To where the west wind wafts the lover's sigh,
From vales where summer streams for ever flow,
Far as where Greenland rears her hills of snow;
From plains where Arab maids are free and fond,
To Sina's [2] daughters and their loveless bond.
Wild must the desert be, and lone the spot,
And cold the wayward heart, where love is not.

O'er Bergia's [3] wall rolls battle's spareless tide,
Fall'n is her glory, and subdued her pride;

---

[2] In Sina, or China, the marriage contract is generally concluded by the parents while the parties are perfect children, and the bridegroom never sees the lady until after the nuptials are celebrated.

[3] The following lines refer to the siege of Bergia, or Hensberg, or Henneberg, in Bavaria, defended by the Duke of Bavaria against the Emperor Guelphus. The town at length capitulated, and the conqueror granted permission to the female inhabitants to escape with as many of their valuables as they could carry. Their heroic conduct on this occasion I have attempted to describe.

O'er Bergia's wall the wing of conquest waves,
No strength that succours, and no arm that saves:
Yet check'd by mercy's voice the warrior stood:
"Shall victory's steel be red with woman's blood?
No! bid them flee, with all they value most,
Ours is no ruffian band nor lawless host;"
Glad were the tidings, and with rapture came,
The bride of yesterday, and matron dame.—
No precious gold nor costly gems they bare,
No robe nor goodly vesture claimed their care.
But, lo! with holy zeal, with generous art,
Each bears her lord, the worshipp'd of her heart.
No arm withstands their path, no foe they fear,
For *he* hath turn'd to hide the softening tear,
To ask if she who gave the parting kiss
Cherish such pure, such sacred love as this!

Such the high sphere where woman's faith should shine,
A flame of purity, a light divine,
Kindling in sorrow, bursting into life
Through pain's thick darkness and the storms of strife;
Her love, the balm by weeping mercy shed
To soothe the broken heart and drooping head.
Not this the star the Roman warrior[*] hail'd,
When beauty strove with valour and prevail'd,
Nor this the faith her lawless spirit gave
When kingdoms bowed to him, and *he* her slave.

[*] The memorable defeat of Antony in the Gulf of Actium, and its subsequent fatalities, through the flight of Cleopatra, are well known. "Though the lips of a strange woman drop as the honeycomb, her end is bitter as wormwood, sharp as a two-edged sword."

But wild, and strange, and wayward was the flame
That mark'd her path, and led the way to shame.
To glory's tomb, and hope's expiring pang,
A sting more bitter than the aspen [5] fang.

And lives there one whose demon-heart can seek
To steal the blush of truth from woman's cheek?
To make the light of earth's most lovely state
A name to scoff at, and a thing to hate?
Be his the joy the serpent tempter felt,
No voice to charm him, and no tear to melt;
Be his the soul no love, no peace can bless,
Despair his portion, for his curse, success.
But darker yet the crime, more foul the deed
In nature's soul-taught law, in holy creed,
To lure with fiendish wile the gentle bride,
The wife of gladness, from her loved one's side;
To stain the page of truth with thoughts unblest,
And hatch the serpent in the turtle's nest!
Oh! dark the crime and strange, and woe to him
Who bids the lamp of purity be dim,
Who wrings the tear from young affection's eye,
And wakes the worm within that will not die.

Not this the path the youthful Persian [6] trod,
Though his a dark'ning faith and heathen god;

---

[5] [Or *adder's*.—ED.]

[6] It is related by Xenophon, that when Cyrus had taken the wife of Tigranes, Prince of Armenia, captive, her husband, who had just married, and was passionately fond of her, offered his own life as the ransom of her liberation. Cyrus was so struck with the generosity of this proposal, that he released the fair bride to her husband, after having treated her during her captivity with the utmost delicacy and honour.

For him there shone not love's all-gladdening ray,
But virtue smiled, and hallow'd was his way;
And there he reign'd o'er many a princely throng,
Lord of his passions, a command more strong.
Oh! 'twas a lovely sight to see that bride,
Who pined for *one* nor lov'd the world beside,
Led forth by him, the high, the lordly youth,
The chief of nations, but the slave of truth.
And whence is he who comes that pair to meet,
With eyes of fearing and with trembling feet,
Who scans with look of dread that maiden's face,
As if for guilty blush, or spoiler's trace?
Oh! none need ask that saw the heaving breast,
The grateful glance which scarcely love repress'd,
Who mark'd the quivering lip that could not speak,
The tear of gladness, and the bloodless cheek!

Woe to the Circean glance, the truthless smile
Of her whose love is strange, whose ways are guile!
Woe to the foot that treads in pleasure's bower,
Nor heeds the serpent coil'd beneath the flower!
To her the dark with guilt, the fallen so low,
That purity is hate, and virtue woe!—
Alas! that she whose very smile is balm,
All that in strife can soothe or sorrow calm,
That she, the child of innocence and love,
Sent as a star, a herald from above,
Should draw the veil of shame around her head,
And walk with men as worms among the dead.

Yon murmuring stream that flows so gently by,
While minstrel willows o'er its waters sigh,

Spreads to the arching sky its mirror tide,
And shows the face of heaven in imaged pride.
Each beaming star that distant ages gave
Saw its bright semblance in that silvery wave,
And now no cloud can tremble on the hill,
But there its darkness is reflected still!
'Tis thus with woman's mind—in every clime
Pure with affection's light, or dark with crime;
The bower of virtue and the home of vice,
A venom'd waste, and fruitful paradise,
The fount whence every gentler feeling flows,
The fire where tameless passion springs and glows;
'Tis hers to bind with faith's all-sacred chain,
Or rend the heart-strings of that faith in twain;
Yes! the thawed snake will sting—the evening dew,
That roses love, will nurse the hemlock too.

Yet life may brighten and the world may bring
Joys born in peace, and hopes that ever spring.
Wealth to allure, and fame with siren tone
Welcoming the pilgrim to her heaven-built throne.
And earth may teem with never-fading flowers,
With blooming palm-wreaths and with rose-clad bowers;
Vain are they all and frail, when sorrows spread
Their veil of darkness round the wanderer's head,
When strife-born chastenings bid the mourner bow,
And pour their vengeance on a lonely brow;
Oh! welcome, lovely then, the home of rest
By peace endear'd, by warm affection blest,
Where all is pure and calm, where all is fair,

As if a seraph held her dwelling there;
Where as on turtle-wings the moments fleet,
And seasons steal away on downy feet.
But night will come, though fair the opening day,
In gloomy pride, and who shall cry, Away!
And those whom youthful life and love have join'd,
Whose hearts were one, like wreaths by nature twin'd,
Even they must sever, and their faith so dear
Leave but a wreck, and plead but for a tear;
Even they must part, and pity's sigh they claim,
Their peace a vapour, and their pride a name.

Alas, for him! the desolated one,
On whom no more will shine affection's sun,
Doom'd the dark flowing, ceaseless tear to shed,
O'er love departed and the lonely bed:
Whose fate it is with weary heart to rove
On memory's wing through bowers which gladness wove,
Where she, the lov'd one, beauty's fairest child,
Gladden'd life's path and every care beguil'd;
Whom youthful passion gave him fond and free,
Who clung to him like ivy round the tree,
Until the spoiler rent her faith away,
And seem'd rejoic'd to grasp so fair a prey!

But flowers bear venom, poison-trees will spring,
In fragrant pride and lovely blossoming;
Sweet is the breeze that wafts the Upas' breath,
And pure the hemlock-stream whose taste is death:
Fair to the stranger came the sacred dove,

That spread her wings and brought him peace and
    love,
Truth rose to him as morning's cloudless bloom,
But passion gather'd like the thunder-womb,
Yet love remain'd though purity was past.
Though sorrow came like plague upon the blast!

*   *   *   *
*   *   *   *

NIGHT.

FAIR Night, I love thy advent! comest thou
    Wrapt in thy diamond-spangled robe of peace,
Or crowned with moonbeams: be thy bosom soft
As youthful love, or wild as wronged affection.
I love thee, Night! when not a summer leaf
Stirs in its place of birth, nor holds communion
With its kindred; and when autumn clouds
Roll at the coming of a tempest like a host
When death pursues them; when the rill of spring
Flows like the vow of innocence to faith,
Pure and unruffled—or the winter stream,
Swoll'n to a flood, is rolling on in strength.
I have been a young pilgrim from the place
Which holds my all of love: and though my staff
Of wandering is but green, I love to think
Upon the hour when my warm heart shall hail

Its vanished home once more.
                        It should be night,
A night of many stars, and pure, and calm,
I would not have a cloud upon the sky
That welcomed me, nor breeze among the trees
Whose smiles should greet my path.
                            Then could I gaze
In all the hope of feeling on that place,
Cradle of many a joy; and I would listen
If all were silent, if the breath of sleep
Broke not upon my ear, to whisper there
That all around was calm and full of peace,
As the blue sky that shaded it.
                           There is a spot
Where I have wandered in my lonely gladness,
And asked for no communion save the link
Which memory cherisht;—and have sought no joy
Save those which hope would bear on fancy's wing;
'Tis a lone rock, and sea-waves swell around
As soft and gently as the heaving bosom
Of matin-beauty at affection's tale!
The moon would throw her light so sweetly there,
As if a seraph came upon each beam
To lave his pinions in the rippling foam,—
I do believe that I should weep, if aught
Had marr'd its beauty, if it did not smile
As when I last was there to sigh farewell.
I love thee, Night! my best affections love thee,
My warmest feelings and my tenderest hopes
Thou hast charmed forth to life; as summer flowers
Will breathe their sweetest fragrance to the breeze

That bears thy dew; and every loathsome thought
Shrinks like the venomous serpent from thy smile,
And coils within its birthplace.
                              Fair thou art,
And dear to youthful lover, to the child
Of nature's poetry; and he whose harp
Bears not a string for thee is one of earth's
Unfavoured sons, a mere existing man!

ON LEAVING HOME.

GOD bless thee! was the last endearing word
   The lip could utter or the heart could feel!
Many did pray for the young exile's weal,
But there was one from whom was only heard,
  God bless thee! and it was affection's knell
  For many a lonely day.
                              The very phrase
Was oft repeated by the parting voice
  Of youthful friendship; and the last farewell
  Of some who loved me in my boyish days
Was warm and tearful.
                              Yet there was but one
Whose heart beat quicker than her eyes ran o'er,
Whose trembling lip refused to whisper more
Than that warm prayer.
                              It was a hallow'd tone.

A TRIBUTE.

PEACE to the memory of the brave!
    He died as warriors ought to die,
His tomb the plain he fought to save,
    His dirge the shout of Victory!
And ne'er in death a nobler slept,
    Nor held the grave a prouder trust,—
He shall not perish there unwept,
    Nor mingle with forgotten dust.

The cypress branch shall mark his tomb
    With friendship's sigh and beauty's tear,
And there the laurel-wreath shall bloom
    O'er deeds to freedom's children dear.
His eagle wing was spread for fame,
    And high on valour's plume he soared,
And history's page shall trace his name
    In minstrel song and high record.

Oh! may the star that set in tears,
    Though bright its dawning was, and fair,
Rise into life in other spheres,
    And shine in holier beauty there.
Peace to the spirit of the brave!
    He died as warriors ought to die,
His tomb the plain he fought to save,
    His dirge the shout of Victory!

ON A WILD VIOLET.

THOU lovely flower! child of the wilderness,
   Giving thy sweetness to the desert's breath,
  Thou art like virtue in this world of death.
In bower or garden we should love thee less
   Than in this wild, uncherished solitude.
   Where nought were beautiful, wert thou not good,
Yea! lovely to the sight.
                Thou art too fair
For dews to nurture long, or winds to spare.
   Thou art so chaste in thy wild innocence
    That it were half profane to tear thee hence.
But heaven's best gifts and earth's least mortal flowers
   Soon fall to dust in this strange world of ours!

LUCRETIA.

LUCRETIA, who shall praise thee? Many hearts
   Have softened at thy tale, and many eyes
Have wept for thee!
              Thou wert a lovely flower
Till a foul worm dared to pollute thy bosom;
And when thou pour'dst thy tarnish'd beauties forth,
Like rose-leaves scattered to the breeze that loved
   them,

SONNET.

A star thou wert, beauteously eminent
In lustrous purity: but a dark cloud
Gathered upon thy brow, and thou didst fall
From the high sphere where none have shone like
    thee;
Thy bosom was the shrine where injur'd faith
Gave innocence a sacrifice to virtue!
Few after thee have seen the rose of love,
And chastity's lily, sisters on a stem,
And partless in their being.
                        Alas! the heat
Of brutish love, beguiled them of their fragrance,
And they did fade.
                    The silver-plumaged bird,
When crime's foul breath defiled her spotless wings,
Closed them for ever.
The voice of whispering calumny did not dare
Breathe of her memory; envy's spotted tongue
Was silent o'er her deathbed; and she fell
Like a young blooming plant before the wind,
With sorrow's blessing.

SONNET.

PURE, lovely fountain! flinging thy white foam
    Like swandown to the wind! dost thou not lave
  Some nymph of beauty with thy silver wave?
Some child of air, making thy breast her home?
  Or murmurest thou sweet music to the breeze

That wantons o'er thy bosom? dost thou woo
Thy fickle lover to be fond and true?
  Or enviest thou the sigh that summer trees
Breathe at his coming? Pure and lovely spring!
  Mermaids might choose thee for their proper dwelling,
  And when the flowers around thy banks are swelling
Forth into beauty, and the mavis' wing
  Hath sought thy own dear willow, there would be
  A scene as fair, as full of harmony,
As that of old where Helle's daughters sung,
And charmed the moonbeams with unearthly tongue.

ON THE "PLEASURES OF MEMORY."

TO him whose soul with strife is rent,
  What gladness can remembrance bring?
The tree that winter storms have bent,
  Revives not with the breath of spring;
  And evening sheds her dews in vain,
  It will not bud nor bloom again.
Though memory dwell on days of peace,
  Our present woes will not be less,
And when our strifes with age increase,
  'Twere well to learn forgetfulness.
  Oblivion's hand might better try
  The heart to soothe—the cheek to dry.

From autumn skies the lightning plays
   On many a withered summer bough,
And thus the joy of happier days
   Shines on the sorrow-wrinkled brow.
Thus memory loves to wander o'er
The spot where she may dwell no more.

THE SEA.

A FRAGMENT.

I LOVE the ocean! from a very child
   It has been to me as a nursing breast,
     Cherishing wild fancies.—
                  I was wont to rest
Gazing upon it, when the breeze was wild,
   And think that every wave reared its white arms
To grasp and chide the wind that rolled along
In fitful buffetings, chanting its hoarse song
   As in stern mockery! Such a scene had charms
For my young heart.
                And when the autumn moon
   Laughed o'er the waters, it was mine to trace
   Her imaged form; as if her tiring-place
Were the wave's bosom, or seeking there some boon
   Of sea-god in his coral bower, she stayed,
Wronging Endymion—then the wind would cease,
And every murmur melt away in peace,

And all be gentle as a softening maid
Breathing love's tell-tale sigh.
                              'Tis said,
In such a night the daughters of the sea
Wake their wild harps in siren minstrelsy;
  And on their crystal-pillow'd couches spread
Their clustering tresses, wooing the young breeze
  To wanton with their ringlets, or whispering tales
Of passionate homage to some chosen star,
Beautifully journeying in its azure car
Through paths of loveliness.
                              Joys such as these,
  Visions of wayless fancy, were the fire
   That burnt within me, and they strung the lyre
My feeble hands have swept.   *   *
      *   *   *   *

A NIGHT-SKETCH.

WRITTEN ON EFFORD DOWN CLIFF,[1] IN THE AUTUMN OF 1820.

DAY sinks upon the wave—the first-born ray
    Of earth's fair lamp is stealing o'er the hill;
It is a night of loveliness—the breeze,
Hush'd on the waters, slumbers like a babe

---

[1] Efford, near Bude in Cornwall, has an old manor-house, partly occupied, in Mr. Hawker's time, as a farm-house, and partly as the occasional residence of Colonel Wrey I'Ans, the father of the first Mrs. Hawker.—ED.

Upon its mother's breast; heaven seems to smile,
And draw its star-gemmed veil in mercy o'er
The deeds of darkness.   'Tis a night of peace,
And the grief-stricken spirit should be forth.
'Tis sweet to be alone on such a night:
The vanisht joys of youth and youthful days,
Borne upon memory's pinions, waken then
The long hushed note of gladness—hope's fair dreams
Whisper of joy, and they will cheat the soul,
And woo us to forgetfulness of self.
The dew is sparkling on the heather-bell,
Pure as the griefless tear that dims the eye
Of sleeping childhood, and the night-bird's song
Breaks on the holy loneliness of earth,
Like seraph's music o'er the slumbering dead!
The exiled wanderer, at an hour like this,
Loves the wild beauty of the mountain brow;
And he will comfort him that the same beam
Which meets his gaze, shines on the distant land,
The dwelling of his fathers.
                              'Tis a night
When nought unhallowed dares to be abroad;
Guilt crouches in its den and shuns the view
Of the bright gladness which it cannot mar.
Pure in her loveliness the evening rose
In playful fondness wooes the moonbeam's glance,
Which seeks not to retire; as beauty's eye
Courts the dear smile it fain would seem to shun.
There is a goodly oak upon the hill,
Which many a winter's blast hath smote in vain,
The fathers of the forest once were there,

And twined their boughs in joyfulness around;
The tender ivy built herself a bower,
Among its branches,—
                    They are with the dust,
But still it lifts its head in aged strength,
And proudly glories in its solitude!
Fair is the moonbeam o'er that lonely tree
As when its brow was green in youthful pride;
So in the dawn of life, and o'er the grave
Of all that made life dear, shines on alike
The peace of heaven.

THE COSSACK'S ADIEU.

PRIDE of my spirit! farewell to thy beauty,
    The war-trump hath blown, and thy Cossack
        must go:
Though affection would silence the summons of duty,
    What warrior would hear not the call of the foe?

I leave thee, my love, for the bosom of danger,
    And dear thy fair image in death as in life;
But it shall not be said in the land of the stranger
    That the race of the Danube were last in the strife.

Nay, weep not, thou dear one, nor banish in sorrow
    The hope that should whisper of victory now;
For the gloom of to-day may be brighten'd to-morrow,
    And who should rejoice in my laurels but thou?

Bound on, my brave steed, and be proud in thy glory,
  For thy hoofs shall be red with the blood of the slain.
Should the deeds of thy master be cherish'd in story,
  Thou wilt not have braved the wild battle in vain.

I may not return to my father's dear dwelling,
  But breathe forth my soul on the steel of the foe,
But when sorrow is there, and her tear-drop is swelling,
  Remember my spirit shrank not from the blow.

Farewell, love. In vain for thy Cossack thou weepest,
  His heart will adore thee as ever it hath.
Plunge on, my proud barb! where the death-groans are deepest,
  And woe to the arm that is raised in thy path!

THE FADED ROSE.

THERE was a rose of nature's choicest growth,
    Meet for the night-bird's home or fairy bower;
The breeze would sigh around it as 'twere loth
    To bear the perfume from so sweet a flower.
The dew of evening loved it, and the ray
    Of fading moonbeams sought its latest smile.
Ye would have deem'd that it could not decay,
    So loved, so sweetly nurtured, but the guile
Of autumn night-winds stole its bloom away:

It died, and morning found a dewy gem
  Hung as in mockery on the withered stem!
And there was one, a lonely, lovely one,
  Who faded like that flower; the blast of grief
(Though sigh nor 'plaining word was heard by none),
  Of very bitterness that mocked relief,
Breathed on her beauty's flower, and leaf by leaf
It fell to nothingness. Some thought she strove
With that unslumbering serpent, blighted love.

A REMEMBRANCE.

SMILES have been mine, and gentle hearts have
    yearned
In love toward me in my pilgrimage!
And there was one, whose smile was valued more
By my young soul than all the common lurings,
The snares of beauty for unpractised feeling.
More suns had shone on her than had been mine
By many a summer; but she still was fair,
And every charm was mellowed into sweetness.

Her form rose up in grace, and not a feature
Bloomed in her loveliness that was not soul:
Her voice was harmony's spirit, and the soft,
Mellifluous breathings of her fairy lip
Were like the air-harp's music, and the sound
Of waters murmuring, in mingled sweetness.

In scenes where hearts beat high and eyes were bright,
Where common love and joy were found in union,
She would sit silent, in delight's abstraction,
Communing with her feelings, wrapt in dreams
Of fancy's vision, and she would be sad
That all around her was—reality.
'Twas said that many strove to gain the heart
Bestowed on none—they could not love like her.

I went to say farewell, before the world
Knew of my footsteps.—
                        'Twas a summer eve,
And day was melting into chastened beauty:
I found her in her bower, her place of life,
A spot that overlooked the wrathless ocean:
She bade me gaze upon a swelling wave,
That rushed unbridled on—a frowning rock
Reared in its path, and it was lost in foam!
Another came in gentleness, and soft
It glided by in silvery loveliness;
"And this," she said, "is life," and as she spake
A tear was trembling in her eloquent eye.
" Thy way is all before thee, and thy path
" None can point out : but may the peace of heaven
" Be to thy goings a star of light!"
She prest my forehead with her trembling lip,
And was to me no more.

I could not leave that place of many thoughts
Till I had wept.

THE ROSE OF THE VALLEY.

CYDWELEW! Cydwelew! thy beauty is o'er
    And the Rose of the Valley will flourish no more.
The spring may return, and the summer may beam
Through the mist of the hill and the spray of the stream,
On flowrets as sweet and on roses as fair,
But the pride of thy loveliness will not be there.
We will weep for thee, Ellen, though tears are in vain,
And the rose that is withered will bloom not again,
Though the joys that are gone we may never recall,
And the love be departed that hallowed them all:
We will weep for thee, Ellen, and mourn for the hour
That saw thy young beauty a withering flower!
The dews may descend, and their softness will bring
The favour of heaven to the blossoms of spring,
And the breeze of the evening, when earth is at rest,
Will woo the young rosebud to open her breast.
But the Rose of the Valley will flourish no more,
And Cydwelew will weep that its beauty is o'er!

A DREAM.

I HAD a dream—a dream of happiness,
    And when I rose up in my bed to bless
Him who had given it, my heart was glowing
With fancy's warmth, and tears of joy were flowing.

A DREAM.

Methought that I was wandering in a land
I know not, and no voice, no hand,
   Guided me in my path—but yet I went
Where earth was lovely, where fresh flowers were
      springing
Forth in their joyfulness, where birds were singing,
   And beautiful rainbows in their richness blent
Formed the sweet sky above me.
                     A bower appeared
Twined with spring roses, and an olive reared
Her tender brow, and branches weeping dew
In soft luxuriance—bending vine-trees grew
   Around that place of loveliness, and hung
Sheltering their clusters from the midlight beam.
A stream of peace, a clear and sparkling stream,
   Flowed on its gentle course—though kingbirds sung,
And willows kissed its waves to woo their stay.
   It seemed a dove came near on trembling wing,
And sought my bosom, and she nestled there
   In peace, as if she were afraid to spring
Again on high—as if the fowler's snare
   Were spread for her—

    *   *   *   *   *
    *   *   *   *   *

My dream is gone! but often still I hear
That stream's sweet music murmuring in my ear,
And feel that dove draw near my softening heart,
As she would cling there, never to depart.

MEMORY.

THERE are moments in life which we cannot forget,
   Which for ever in memory's brightness shine on.
Though they seem to have been but to teach us regret,
   And to sadden our hearts when their beauty is gone.
But still they are fountains of blessing that flow,
   Like the spring in the desert, to freshen our path;
They are streamlets of peace in this valley of woe
   When the flowers of gladness are blighted in wrath.

There are joys over which the fond spirit hath sighed,
   And in bitterness found that its sighs were in vain;
As the roses of summer will bloom in their pride,
   But to tell us how soon they will wither again.
And yet there are some which cannot be effaced,
   Which in peace and in strife will for ever be dear,
And without them this life were a thorn-bearing waste,
   Too dark for a smile, and too vain for a tear!

It is said that the nightingale cannot forget
   The spot whence her wild wing first bore her away,
But when evening draws near she will warble there yet,
   And more soft is her note and more tender her lay.
She will love not the valley and seek not the hill,
   And though she may wander, it will not be long,
For when spring fades at last she is singing there still,
   Till her death-note is breathed in the birthplace of song.

And the harp which the love-wing of feeling hath
    swept
  Will memory waken and hallow its strain,
And to hearts that have mourned and to eyes that
    have wept,
  The voice of its sweetness will not be in vain.
For in moments of suffering it whispers of peace,
  Like music which none but the dying may hear,
As the song of the nightingale never will cease,
  But will always be sweetest when darkness is near.

SHAKESPEARE.

A FRAGMENT.

I SAW thee, Shakespeare, in a morning dream,
    Seated upon a throne—beautiful spirits
Ministered unto thee, and lovely songs
They murmur'd in thy ear.
                        First Fancy came
In cherubine sweetness—braidless her soft hair,
Unzoned her robe; and yet in every tress,
In every wantoning fold, there was a charm
Of natural chastity.
                    She drew near
Delicately, like maiden to her lover,
And with a smile of dimpling witchery
She said, thou wast her own dear love, the first,
The chosen one her youth delighted in!

Then with harmonious step came Music nigh,
Bearing a broken harp; and aye she swept
Its varying chords, mingling irregular notes
Into a lay of sweetness—and she told thee
'Twas thine own harp—with all its fairy breathings
Sacred to thee! and dearer to her heart
Than all the measured cadences of song.

* * * * *
* * * * *

TO NATURE.

NATURE, I love thee! in thy varying form,
    Soft with the dew, and maddening with the storm;
The wild wind struggling with the tameless sea,
The zephyr murmuring in the greenwood tree;
I love thee, Nature, from the withered leaf
That falls the tribute tear of autumn grief,
To the proud forest clad by summer-love,
Calm in its bed, but rock'd by winds above!
Spirit of song! the minstrel's nurturing breast,
Where is thy dwelling, where thy place of rest?
Lov'st thou the fountain of the autumn rill,
When breezes slumber, and the birds are still?
Or soarest thou when thunder's womb is rent,
On eagles' pinions through the firmament?

TO NATURE.

Dost thou not wander through the peaceless sky,
Its fire the lightning of thy meteored eye?
Dost thou not fly where ocean tempests are,
Tread on the waves, and veil the evening star?
Thou dost, fair queen! I see thy image rise,
Poised on the earth, and grasping at the skies,
Around thy brow the clouds of evening meet,
And morning flowers are opening at thy feet,
Blent with the hues of earth thy broidered vest,
The tints of heaven soft mingling o'er thy breast,
Lovely thy dwelling-place, thy throne of air,
For beauty ministers a handmaid there!
There's not a flower that summer suns can warm
That does not bless thee for its meted charm;
There's not an autumn breeze that wantons by
Which bears not music from thy whispered sigh.
All love thee, Nature, from the Switzer-maid,
Culling thy blossoms for a ringlet-braid,
To the proud Arab girl with loosened hair,
Winning thy fragrant breath a bridegroom there!

Yes! Art may gild with bright and varied beam
The sculptor's vision and the painter's dream,
But thou art fairer on thy own green sod
Than Luxury templed with her Dagon-god:
Thy smiles are brighter where young roses spring
Than all that imaged loveliness can bring!
To pride's high dwelling—glory's pillared dome,
Ruin will fly and claim a Samson tomb.
But where thy robe is mantling o'er the hill,
Sunbeams and flowers will shine and blossom still.

TO NATURE.

Where chieftains dwelt the ivy-wreaths have grown,
And foxes earth'd beneath the sculptured stone.
Where goblets circled and where minstrels sung,
The midnight bird is nestling o'er her young!

* * * * *

Heard ye the eagle screaming on the blast,
As o'er her plumes the quivering lightning passed?
The rain-drops sound, the music of the rill,
The breeze awakening on the eastern hill?
Saw ye the wild-bird droop his wing of fear?
The earth is listening if the storm be near—
There stirs no leaf, there floats no wavy cloud,
And yet the distant fountain's gush is loud!
These are thy charms, fair Nature, this the scene,
Where, like the Tishbite's robe, thy soul hath been,
Breath'd thy sweet sigh, and shed thy gentle tear,
O'er gladness clinging to the breast of fear!
Oh! thou art lovely in thy storms of night,
Thy rainless clouds that herald summer light,
Thy stars sweet shining, and thy suns of fire,
Thy breezy music and proud tempest lyre!

And I will hail thee, love thee as the flower
Loves the young night-wind and the morning shower;
For thou hast nurtured me, and thine the breast
My infant minstrel lips in fear have prest,
And thine the voice that cheered my trembling way,
To song's high shrine with boyhood's tribute-lay.

AN INSCRIPTION FOR AN AGED OAK.

COME hither, stranger! I would commune with
  thee!
Art thou but young? but tender in thy years?
I was a sapling once, and bent my brow
To every breath of heaven that greeted me!
They pass me now, and scarcely move the leaf
That stronger winds have left.
                         There was a time
When the soft zephyring spring came joyfully,
Like a young bride, with bloom upon her cheek—
And mine her earliest smile; but she is fled
To her young loves, and scorns my hoary locks.
Learn, then, that friendship passeth as the wind,
That love will fade: and trust thou not in man!
But art thou stricken with departed years,
And bent beneath their burden?
                         Nearer yet
I bid thee come, there's sympathy between us.
The warmth of many summer suns hath beamed
In kindliness upon me—many dews
Have wept their freshening influence on my leaf.
But now the flowers that spring up at my root
Upbraid my shadeless branches; for the heat
Shines in its parching strength and withers them.
Hast thou a child, old man? Bid him come here,
And I will tell him what it is to live
An isolated thing without a bond

Spun from affection's web; without a tie,
Though but of flax, to bind him to the earth.
And he shall cherish thee, old man, and heed
Even the poor counsel of an aged tree!

DIANA.

STAR of the buskined goddess! chastely shining
   Among the highborn children of the skies!
  Thou'rt like the stolen glance of bashful eyes,
Making love, fear; and timidly divining
From half-breathed words the wish they dare not
    know.
  Thou loveliest light that steals down from above!
  And could'st thou tell young feeling not to love
Thy spirit-kindling smile? It is as though
  The rose should whisper that she is not fair,
  And scorn the amorous night-bird's vesper-prayer;
It is as if the summer wind should blow
  Delayed with fragrance, and in pride declare
It breathes no sweetness. Beauty loves thy ray,
  Fair star! for thou dost tremble in the sky
  As if in fear lest some unholy eye
Should mock with wanton glance thy stainless way!

TO AMA.

THOU canst not, when the night's own beam
    Is trembling o'er the summer stream
Bid its charm'd ray be ever fair,
And shine in fadeless beauty there.

And when the rippling sea's at rest
And sunlight slumbers on its breast,
Thou canst not make its shining stay,
Nor bind with love one western ray.

But thou canst woo the star of truth
To beam upon thy gentle youth,
And that will shine, and that will stay,
Though love and gladness fleet away.

AN EPITAPH ON A YOUNG LADY.

FROM THE FRENCH.

FAREWELL! farewell! Like flowers that wither,
    Thou'st fled upon the wing of death,
And love and sorrow flew together,
    To bear away thy parting breath!

Pain's gentlest tear was sorrow weeping
    That thus thy blossoming promise fled,
While love his holiest shaft was steeping
    In the warm tears that sorrow shed.

"WHAT LOVEST THOU?"

I LOVE the song of tender feeling
    Fair lips begin;
I love soft eyes of light, revealing
    The soul within.

I love the lark of summer, winging
    Its song-cheered way;
And dear to me the mavis, singing
    Her evening lay.

Sweet is the violet returning
    To starlit sleep;
And fair the rosebud of the morning,
    Where dewdrops weep.

I seek the stream of gentle flowing,
    Where suns are bright;
And hail the chastened moon bestowing
    Her silver light.

I trace the shades of sunset, fleeting
    O'er the blue tide;
And dancing waves the day-beam meeting
    As if in pride.

I seek the spot where fairies dancing
    Have traced their path
(When midnight stars are brightly glancing)
    To tempt their wrath.

Lady, there's not a light ray streaming
From skies above,
On earth there's not a flowret beaming
I do not love!

INTRODUCTORY AND FAREWELL ADDRESSES.

The following lines were written to be recited as Introductory and Farewell Addresses at the Public Examination of Mr. Tucker's Pupils, at Ham House, Charlton-Kings. The repetition of the latter depended, of course, on the success it anticipated.

INTRODUCTORY ADDRESS.

" Concurritur."—HOR.

HARD is the task, ill fit for youthful days,
To gain from judgment's voice the meed of of praise,
And deep the pain that youthful souls must feel,
When censure damps the glow of early zeal.
The flower that dies before the eastern gale,
Once promised fragrance to its native vale,
And many a bud that genius hailed her own,
Reproof hath blighted ere its tints were known.
Knew ye the joy your cherished smiles will give,
While life shall brighten or remembrance live;
Knew ye how valued, nay, how loved by youth,
Its first-gained laurel from the lip of truth:
Then would ye not withhold the approving smile,
The cheap-bought recompense of youthful toil.

We all may leave these scenes of happiness,
To welcome joy or sink beneath distress.
But school-boy pleasures and the much-loved spot
Where once they flourished, ne'er will be forgot;—
Should happiness be ours, or fortune bring
Life's dearest blessings on her welcome wing,
Proud shall we be to drop the gentle tear,
And midst our joys to own their birth-place, *here!*
Should sorrow haunt the evening dreams of life,
And tears be mingled with the cup of strife,
Still shall your smiles be traced on memory's page,
To gladden manhood, and to soothe old age!
As the young fledgling leaves its mother's breast,
And flies the covert of the sheltering nest,
To track with feeble wing the untried air,
And find its safety or destruction there:
Behold *us* now with anxious hearts draw near,
Hope in our souls, though not unmixed with fear.
Yet will we trust that not in vain we plead
That candour may prevail, and youth succeed;
And long 'twill be our first, our dearest pride,
Should praise await our toil where *you* preside.

Farewell Address.

"Victoria læta."—Hor.

'TWERE vain to whisper what we all must feel,
   The joy of heart, the proud success of zeal;
And vain the gratitude our lips could pay
For the high triumph we have won to-day!

The wreath of praise your generous smiles have twined
Around each youthful heart shall memory bind,
The gentler feelings of that heart to share,
And long to bloom in fadeless beauty there.
Dear will our triumph be, and doubly dear,
Since we have won our first-born laurels *here;*
Well may applause like yours the heart beguile,
And Fear be mute, when Judgment deigns to smile:
Proud is the conquest when the victors gain
A prize so often sought and sought in vain!
Take with you, then, in fervency, in truth,
The cheerful gratitude of guileless youth.
Cloth'd in no glozing phrase, no practis'd art,
The pure unmingled incense of the heart.
The high-born boast, " we did not vainly sue "
The generous praise our feeble efforts drew,
Speak to the soul, and justly, deeply tell,
Vain is our gratitude, and thus, farewell!

"THE AXE IS LAID AT THE ROOT OF THE TREE."

THE Chieftain is fallen! and in anguish of spirit,
    The vial of vengeance is poured on his head;
Let his fate then atone for the wrath he may merit,
    And pity a tear to his memory shed.

THE AXE IS LAID AT THE ROOT OF THE TREE.

Though freedom rejoice, and her children may glory
  In the valour that laid the proud enemy low,
Yet it shall not be read in the page of her story,
  That England could smile at the death of a foe.

When the pride of the forest is blighted and perished,
  We mourn for the whirlwind that breathed on its bud,
But the garlands of conquest, the laurels he cherished,
  Were planted in slaughter and watered with blood.
And soon were they withered and laid in the furrow,
  O'er liberty's birthplace to bloom not again,
And the arm of her children soon plucked them in sorrow
  From the brow of the warrior, who wreathed them in vain.

Yet, though dark his proud soul with the lust of ambition,
  Though banish'd his name from the lips of the brave,
Let us hope that his solitude cherished contrition,
  Let the voice of his crimes be unheard from the grave!
It behoves not the mighty to crush the defeated,
  Nor to trample the brow which is laid in the dust,
And the measure of woe that for him hath been meted,
  Claims from mercy a sigh in the hearts of the just.

The warrior is fallen—and low lies the proud-hearted,
  And the sigh of oblivion is passed from the brave,
The warrior is fallen—and his pride is departed,
  To mingle with earth and to reign in the grave.

And Conquest shall mourn for the victim she nourish'd,
  And weep for the soul that was breathed at her feet,
For his laurels but bloom'd and their glory but flourish'd
  To render the pride of the victor more sweet.

DAVID'S LAMENT.

LET the voice of the mourner be heard on the mountain,
  And woe breathe her sigh over Besor's blue wave,
Upon Gilboa's hill there is opened a fountain,
  And its fast-flowing stream is the blood of the brave!
Oh! dry be that hill from the rains of the morning,
  On its brow may no dew of the evening fall,
But the warriors of Israel from conquest returning
  View herbless and withered the death-place of Saul!
From the borders of Judah let gladness be banish'd,
  Ye maidens of Israel be deep in your woe,
For the pride of the mighty in battle is vanish'd
  The chief of the sword, and the lord of the bow.
And long shall the chieftains of Gilead deplore them,
  And mourn the dark fate of the high and the brave,
The song of the minstrel will oft be breath'd o'er them,
  And holy the tear that shall fall on their grave.

"IS NATURE COME TO THIS?"

THERE was a man who died with rage—they said
It was a fearful sight—his spirit fled
In hate and cursing, and no tears were shed
By those around.   The oaths came rolling forth
Like fire from a volcano—and they forced
Their way with difficulty through the throat,
Which seemed with very hellishness to burst,
Till with one inward-breathed and deep-drawn note,
He howled his last.   And when he sank to earth,
All turned away—they could not bear to look
Upon the dreadful page of nature's book
Which lay before them—wherein hearts might read
In words of fire, how many a loathsome deed
Of strange, unholy darkness must have been
Before the world could bring forth so much sin!

DEBORAH'S SONG.

WARRIORS of Israel! sheathe the sword,
    And dash the waving plume away,
With triumph spread the festal board,
    And shout on high the joyful lay.

DEBORAH'S SONG.

Fallen is the pride of Jabin's host,
   And ceased the triumph of the foe;
Yet let not Israel's warriors boast,
   A *woman's* hand hath dealt the blow.

Frail though by nature woman be,
   Ill fit to lift the avenging rod,
Yet is her soul from weakness free,
   And strong, the instrument of God.
Loud is the wail in Jabin's band,
   And deep the woe their souls must feel.
Where is their chief's resistless hand?
   Where his proud arm and vengeful steel?

He died a death that none should die,
   Whate'er their deeds, whate'er their guilt,
His pangs were dear to woman's eye,
   By woman's hand his blood was spilt:
For him no hostile bow was bent,
   For him was drawn no foeman's sword:
His death-place was the peaceful tent,
   His death, the judgment of the Lord!

TRANSLATION

OF AN EPITAPH ON ROSA, COUNTESS OF WARWICK, IN BROADHIMSON CHURCHYARD.

ROSE of the world! thy tender bloom
    Will live no more in earthly bower,
The grave hath drank the sweet perfume
    Which once was thine, thou lovely flower!
Yet thou hast left this place of tears,
    To breathe in sweetness purer air,
For thou shalt bloom in happier spheres,
    And none shall steal thy fragrance there!

INSCRIPTION, CARVED IN STONE, OVER THE PORCH DOOR OF THE VICARAGE HOUSE, MORWENSTOW.

A House, a Glebe, a Pound a Day;[1]
A Pleasant Place to Watch and Pray.
Be True to Church—Be Kind to Poor,
O Minister! For Evermore.

[1] The annual value of the vicarage rentcharge.—R. S. H.

THE END.

www.ingramcontent.com/pod-product-compliance
Lightning Source LLC
Chambersburg PA
CBHW021203230426
43667CB00006B/539